11·17·77

A SCORNFUL
WONDER

A SCORNFUL WONDER

WONDER

What's Right
with the Church

C. LESLIE GLENN

David McKay Company, Inc.

NEW YORK

Library of Congress Cataloging in Publication Data

Glenn, C. Leslie, 1900–1976
  A scornful wonder.

  1. Church. 2. Christian life
I. Title.
BX1746.G55   261.1   77–5712
ISBN 0–679–50740–X

10 9 8 7 6 5 4 3 2 1

To the Blessed Memory of
Pope John XXIII,
Pontifex, Maker of Bridges

CONTENTS

Contents

PREFACE

With a Word About Putdowns

All work and no plagiarism makes Jack a dull preacher. That's a viewpoint that can be used to support an important rule in sermons: don't constantly give your sources. The preacher tells what he learns from people, books, press and TV, prayer, and life itself. It is not important that he be original, only that he repeat the truth as far as he sees it. It bothers the congregation if he keeps interrupting with:

"As the late Reinhold Niebuhr put it . . ."

"Saint Augustine (not of Canterbury, but of Hippo) tells us . . ."

"Three weeks ago last Tuesday, George F. Will wrote in his column . . ."

Such remarks can be distracting; sermons must race on with no asides.

But published work is different. In books it is embarrassing if the sources of good ideas and phrases are not acknowledged, because everybody knows the author couldn't write that well himself. Modesty compels ascription even if the copyright laws do not. So in this book I try to give references. A more important reason for telling who said it first is to lure the reader into the original books, in which the English is better. *Protestantism in*

Pidgin English was my first secret title, thinking to make a joke out of necessity. The final version is dedicated to Pope John XXIII, which says something.

My last secret title dawned on me as I read and reread what I had written:

The Religious Thought
of
Thornton Niven Wilder
1897–1975
From his Books, Letters,
and Conversations

If the Bible is quoted on every page, this dear friend is quoted on every second page, generally without credit. I was astonished when I realized how many ideas and phrases originally came from him. His friendship for fifty years has been not only a joy but an inspiration, a word he wouldn't have liked. When he died in December 1975, his sister told me she thought his greatest concern was writing letters to friends, not his books or plays. He cared deeply for people, one by one.

All of us, whoever or wherever we are, have noticed that what happens inside a church is often dismissed as ritualism or meaningless mumbo-jumbo. This criticism discourages the faint-hearted, for whom any putdown can paralyze a practice. The tough-minded have exactly the opposite temper; they look twice at anything that is given a "bad mouth." To encourage this bold second look, I have given each chapter a one-word title that is a putdown for the practice recommended in that chapter: like "RITUALISM" for not forgetting the inside of a church; "MYSTICISM" for being drawn toward God; and "DO-GOODISM" for caring for neighbor.

Some of the terms used for chapter headings have always been putdowns; others are noble titles fallen on evil days. All have the contradictory effect of weakening the timid and strengthening the valiant, as we sing in "The Church's One Foundation":

> Though with a scornful wonder
> Men see her sore opprest,
> By schisms rent asunder,
> By heresies distrest;
> Yet saints their watch are keeping,
> Their cry goes up, "How long?"
> And soon the night of weeping
> Shall be the morn of song.

The idea for this book came to me two decades ago when I was on the staff of the Mental Health Research Institute of the University of Michigan Medical School in Ann Arbor. I am greatly indebted to scholarly friends who checked the theology, sociology, and other learned subjects. Many other kind manuscript readers (believers and unbelievers) and a superb editor have helped enormously. I have also been encouraged constantly by the members of the only two parishes I served and by the people of Washington Cathedral, where the book was finished this summer on the Feast of the Transfiguration.

August 6, 1976   C.L.G.

The Rev. Dr. C. Leslie Glenn, sub-dean of the Washington Cathedral, former rector of Christ Church, Cambridge, Massachusetts, and St. John's, Lafayette Square (known as "the Church of the Presidents"), died at age 76 of a heart attack, on November 8, 1976, in Washington, D.C.—*Ed.*

ACKNOWLEDGMENTS

For permission to use extracts from the works cited below, grateful acknowledgment is made to the following publishers and copyright owners:

John Baillie, *The Sense of the Presence of God*, (The Gifford Lectures 1961–62), Charles Scribner's Sons. By permission.

Stephen Vincent Benet, *John Brown's Body*, Holt, Rinehart and Winston, Inc. Copyright 1927, 1928 by Stephen Vincent Benet, renewed 1955, 1956 by Rosemary Carr Benet. Reprinted by permission of Brandt & Brandt.

John Betjeman, "Christmas" from *Collected Poems*, John Murray Ltd. and Houghton Mifflin Co. By permission.

Louis Bouyer, *The Spirit and Forms of Protestantism*, Newman Press, 1961.

G. K. Chesterton, *Orthodoxy*, The Bodley Head, Ltd. By permission.

E. E. Cummings, *Poems 1923–1924*. Copyright 1950 by E. E. Cummings. Reprinted from his volume *Complete Poems 1913–1962* by permission of Harcourt Brace Jovanovich, Inc.

Pierre Teilhard de Chardin, *The Divine Milieu*. Copyright 1960 by Harper & Row. By permission.

Robert Frost, from "Kitty Hawk" in *The Poetry of Robert Frost*, edited by Edward Connery Lathem. Reprinted by permission of Holt, Rinehart and Winston, Publishers.

Roger Lancelyn Green and Walter Hooper, *C. S. Lewis: A Biography*, Harcourt Brace Jovanovich, Inc. By permission.

Michael P. Hamilton, editor, *The Charismatic Movement*, Wm. B. Eerdmans Publishing Co. Used by permission.

Rudyard Kipling, *Rudyard Kipling's Verse*, Doubleday & Company, Inc.

Phyllis McGinley, *Times Three*. Copyright 1958 by Phyllis McGinley. Reprinted by permission of The Viking Press.

Samuel Eliot Morison, *The European Discovery of America: The Southern Voyages, 1492–1616*, Oxford University Press.

Daniel P. Moynihan, *Coping: On the Practice of Government*. Copyright 1973 by Daniel P. Moynihan. Reprinted by permission of Random House, Inc.

Gilbert Murray, *Five Stages of Greek Religion*, Beacon Press.

E. V. Rieu, *The Four Gospels: A New Translation from the Greek*. By permission of Penguin Books Ltd.

George Santayana, *The Last Puritan*. Copyright 1935–1936 by Charles Scribner's Sons. By permission.

Albert Schweitzer, *The Quest of the Historical Jesus*, Published in the U.S. by Macmillan Publishing Co., Inc. Reprinted with permission of Macmillan Publishing Co., Inc.

George Bernard Shaw, *Saint Joan*, The Society of Authors on behalf of the Bernard Shaw Estate.

Willard L. Sperry, *Strangers and Pilgrims*, Little, Brown and Company.

William Temple, *Nature, Man and God*. (The Gifford Lectures 1932–33 and 1933–34), by permission of Macmillan, London and Basingstoke and St. Martin's Press.

Abram Tertz, *The Makepeace Experiment*, translated by Manya Harari. Copyright 1965 by Harvill Press & Random House Inc. Permission by Pantheon Books, a Division of Random House, Inc.

Baron Friedrich Von Hugel, *Selected Letters, 1896–1924*. Reprinted by permission of the publishers, E. P. Dutton & Co., Inc.

Alfred N. Whitehead, *Adventures of Ideas*. Copyright 1933 by Macmillan Publishing Co., Inc., renewed 1961 by Evelyn Whitehead. Reprinted with permission of Macmillan Publishing Co., Inc.

L. Pearce Williams, *Michael Faraday: A Biography*. Copyright Chapman & Hall Ltd., Basic Books, Inc., Publishers, New York.

Amos Wilder, *The Healing of the Waters*. Copyright 1943 by Harper and Row Publishers, Inc. By permission of the Publisher.

William Butler Yeats, "A Prayer for My Daughter," from *Collected Poems*, Copyright 1924 by Macmillan Publishing Co., Inc., renewed 1952 by Georgia Yeats. Reprinted with permission of Macmillan Publishing Co., Inc.

William Butler Yeats, "A Prayer for Old Age," from *Collected Poems*, Copyright 1934 by Macmillan Publishing Co., Inc., renewed 1962 by Georgia Yeats. Reprinted with permission of Macmillan Publishing Co., Inc.

A SCORNFUL
WONDER

FALSTAFF: If I have forgotten what the inside of a church is made of, I am a peppercorn, a brewer's horse: the inside of a church! Company, villainous company, hath been the spoil of me.

—*Shakespeare*, Henry IV, Part I

One

RITUALISM

Not Forgetting the Inside of a Church

" 'Man does not live by bread alone,' and that's all I'll say."
But when the distinguished psychoanalyst said it four
times in the course of his medical paper, he naturally was
asked in the discussion why he never finished the quotation, "but by every word that proceedeth out of the mouth
of the Lord doth man live" (*Deuteronomy* 8:3).

"I don't like the Saint James Version," he replied. "Besides, I'm uncertain about God. I stop at 'man does not live
by bread alone'; every doctor is sure of that much, and
that's as far as I'll go."

Then he did go further by asking his audience to think of
substitutes for "every word of the Lord." I volunteered the
word "information" because it had a scientific sound, and
he quickly agreed (a little too quickly, as I discovered):
Man does not live by bread alone, but by information does
man live. So science and religion had another reconcilia-
tion, that man lives by meat and potatoes plus information.
A few days later, he startled me with one sentence on a
post card:

"By the way, what is the information?"

How to answer such a question? List a five-foot shelf of
books on history, science, and philosophy followed later by

half a dozen theological books? Send a three-page letter, single spaced? Give a tract from the church porch?

By accident I found out how to answer a few evenings later when a senator from Vermont stood on the handkerchief-sized lawn in my back yard and pronounced one word:

"Doom."

"I beg your pardon, sir?" I replied.

"*Doom!*"

"I don't think I understand."

"DOOM!" he shouted.

His wife said, "He means get Doom and put it on the grass. It's a powder."

I bought a can the next day and put some on the lawn. Sure enough, the brown spots disappeared. The fine print on the label gave the chemical name of Doom, when to use it, what grubs it killed, how to make yourself vomit if you swallowed some by accident, *et cetera, et cetera.* But the only information I needed to get going was that one word, *doom.* With like Yankee economy, I wrote on a post card to the psychoanalyst:

"CHURCH."

The only information he needed to get going was that one word. It is certainly a less puzzling word than *doom*; everyone knows what *church* is, that it holds various kinds of meetings (at least nine different kinds), and that everyone is welcome at any of them. He could read the fine print on the label later; as a starter all he had to tell his troubled patients was to go to church.

Church Wedding

The ritualism I'd like to begin with is the wedding because it is the service most commonly attended by nonchurchgoing people, and the source of their knowledge of the

inside of the church. It is also the rite that generates the
most speculation in these days of widespread divorce.

The wedding guest, sitting in church while the organ
plays the prelude, has time for reflection. If he knows the
psychoanalyst's quotation that "man does not live by bread
alone," he may think gloomily that it is even more true of
wedding cake. Yet at the same time he is moved by the
hopefulness of the occasion. Here is fresh evidence of
human courage: these two people mean to have a home.
God knows that is a wonderful thing; God knows it is not
always achieved; God help them. His Name comes into it
naturally; there are as few atheists at weddings as there
were said to be in foxholes. In both situations, the issue is
too desperate. In a foxhole, life or death with intermediate
stages of maiming; in a marriage, happiness or misery in
varying proportions.

It is appropriate that this couple's adventure into the
unknown start in a church. Merely being inside the building for their wedding may lead them into a new habit of
going to church, and the result will be to make them mal-
leable in their married life. Every week the Sunday ritualism tells them that they are sinners, that no one is good
enough for anything (including matrimony), but that with
God they can be different. Church attendance makes people considerate of each other. They may be tired of the
advertising "pray together and stay together," but they
know the truth a wise old aunt tossed off one evening:
"Marriage is partly a matter of door-slamming."

In addition to being exposed to pious billboards and
Aunty's aphorisms, the new husband and wife get support
from Shakespeare. He has Falstaff say, "If I have forgotten
what the inside of a church is made of, I am a peppercorn,
a brewer's horse: the inside of a church!" (*Henry IV, Part
I*). The peppercorn is so small it has long been a symbol of
futility; the brewer's horse in Shakespeare's day had as
much beer in his stomach as on his back, since he was fed

the unsold stock. Today's marriage counselors are confronted with the same old human woes: boredom and escapism. And many agree with Shakespeare's cure—"the inside of a church." He makes Falstaff say it twice, "the inside of a church!"

Another consequence of the church wedding is that it entails a meeting with a minister. This introduction may lead to a relationship that can help the couple if things begin to go wrong in their marriage. A Christian marriage is not what takes place on a certain day during ten minutes (six without music); it is years of background before the wedding—home, Sunday school, neighborhood—and years of continuance afterward. Both before and after the actual ceremony, the clergyman has had a part; scrupulous ones will not marry strangers who come in off the street, and they try to keep up their friendships with those they do marry. They themselves have no illusion that a few words and gestures can cast a spell on the couple to make their relationship foolproof. That would be magical, and a wedding service is sacramental, a sharp difference. In magic the Unseen must obey the secret word or action. "Open Sesame" unfailingly unlocks the cave. Rubbing the lamp compels the genie's release. In a sacrament, there is no compulsion; God's Spirit communicates to man's spirit through matter, and human spirit responds to God through matter, but there is no automatic result either way. God and man are both free agents.

Sacramental marriage is both physical and spiritual. It is an "outward and visible sign of an inward and spiritual grace." The physical consummates the spiritual as the ancient words made plain: "With this ring I thee wed, with my body I thee worship, and with all my worldly goods I thee endow." Physically (and legally) the bride and bridegroom must consent out loud, have at least two witnesses, give and pledge their troth, exchange a ring or rings, and join hands. In medieval weddings, and still in rural places,

the bride and groom are put to bed by the guests to dramatize this point. Most Christians do not hold that sexual
intercourse is a concession to the flesh, allowable only for
the purpose of having children.

The sacramental nature of marriage also makes clear the
reverse, that the spiritual consummates the physical. Only
love gives meaning to sex; the physical by itself is empty;
"coitus without coexistence is demonic" (Karl Barth); God
created Eve for companionship with Adam, not for a casual
liaison; she was not created from Adam's loins but from his
rib. "It is not good that the man should be alone; I will
make him an help meet for him" (*Genesis* 2:18). This
deceptively naïve story was written late in history, even
though it comes early in the Bible. Long before man had a
help meet, "bone of my bones, and flesh of my flesh"
(*Genesis* 2:23), he had troops of women (polygamy), or
the woman had troops of men (polyandry), or everyone
had everyone (promiscuity). Primitive inheritance was
often through the mother because nobody could be sure
who the father was.

If such anthropological reflections occur to the wedding
guest, he may remember Mrs. Antrobus's speech in Thornton Wilder's *Skin of our Teeth* about how it took women
five thousand years to get the ring. The climb toward
woman's present position has been long and slow. Until
Moses's day a man could divorce his wife by simply telling
her to leave, and if he changed his mind later, he could
claim he had never divorced her. Moses improved woman's
position by requiring the man to write out the divorcement
so that at least she would have a written record to prove
she was discarded. Jesus raised the position of woman further by teaching that writing out the divorce was not
enough to condone the action. He said that a man shall
cleave to his wife; and they twain shall be one flesh (*Matthew* 19:5, quoting *Genesis* 2:24).

As for a woman divorcing a man, that was impossible

except under rare circumstances. The equality of the sexes is being realized only gradually in history; as recently as fifty years ago a woman promised to obey her husband, a man to love his wife. In some countries a divorced woman lost property and children and found it difficult to earn a living. For this poor reason, divorces were scarcer in the past; the only choice for a divorced woman was to go back to her father or to starve. As late as 1914, James Barrie's play *The Twelve Pound Look* portrayed a wife who scraped together twelve pounds (then sixty dollars) to buy a typewriter so she could learn stenography and leave a cruel husband. The twelve-pound look is the independent look. Wilder's remark about the ring meant that after five thousand years, woman had won the independence in marriage that man had always had; she has come a long way.

Christians and their Jewish forebears have fought for permanent marriage for five millennia, and they may now be realizing the fruition of this dream: marriage freely entered into and freely continued by both sexes in increasing numbers. On a small scale, it has always existed: Abraham and Sarah, Isaac and Rebecca, Jacob and Rachel are mentioned in old wedding services as instances of happy marriages in Biblical days. These couples were not entirely free from marital troubles (read *Genesis* again for the light it throws on sex). The God of Abraham, Isaac, and Jacob could not save His patriarchs from family difficulties, but their marriages were permanent, as their neighbors' were not. This same try for permanence has been made in Christian and Jewish marriages down through the ages and into the twentieth century. It could be wrong, as some lecturers contend in their enthusiasm for primitive customs; in any event, permanence in the Bible's sense belongs to the future more than to the past.

What is called the sexual revolution is actually a sexual reversion; promiscuity is not advance but retreat. There is nothing novel about "sex-swinging." It is prehistoric. Sex morality is now widely regarded as old-fashioned, but promiscuity and temporary marriage are more old-fashioned than Moses and the Ten Commandments, going back to the earliest records.

Faithfulness and permanence in marriage are coming into fresh possibilities all over the world because of the increased liberation of women. The Church was looking to the far future when it asked husband and wife to "forsake all others" and make the same promise of loyalty, "for better for worse, for richer for poorer, in sickness and in health, to love and to cherish, till death us do part." It is a fantastically difficult promise, yet we believe it is "according to God's holy ordinance," intended when "He which made them at the beginning made them male and female" (*Matthew* 19:4).

It is paradoxical, but high divorce statistics do not demonstrate a disillusionment with marriage. They suggest instead that human beings are seeking permanent marriages instead of transient affairs. In an age when divorce is legally easy and has lost much of its social stigma, the revealing statistics are the number of stable homes and the high proportion of remarriages after divorce. *Time* wrote, "American men seem to have decided that if there is love, only marriage will suffice in the long run, and if there is no love, only boredom can result; thus does life forever invent morality."

A short way to sum it up is to say that the Church does not believe in divorce, a rule of thumb to be held in the mature mind and drilled into the young one. The cynic who said there are few good marriages added that there are no good divorces. So it was deplorable for a mother to say to her ten-year-old daughter, "I gave you no middle name because when you are divorced and remarried you will have too many names." The Church faults parents who tell their children they expect them to make a bad first marriage. One clergyman, later unfrocked, used to ask the bride and groom, "Will you promise . . . so long as ye both shall love one another?" instead of "so long as ye both shall live?" He was reinforcing the Hollywood myth that love comes and goes and what can anyone do? He implied that will power has no part in love, that a promise here has no meaning. These ways of justifying impermanence are from advantaged circles, but prehistoric casualness about marriage exists also among the deprived.

What looks like Church intransigence against divorce recalls Queen Victoria's motto, which Churchill kept on his desk during World War II: "We are not interested in the possibilities of defeat. They do not exist." On the same theory, before the unification of the armed forces, old admirals used to criticize the Army for always having plans for "retreat to a previously prepared position." They said the Navy had no retreat plans and therefore it never retreated. (Actually the Navy has always had an escape contingency known as "getting the hull out of here.") In principle, the Church in marriage never has plans for retreat to a previously prepared position. However, it is not blind to the difficulties of marriage and is a reservoir of wisdom and stability. It also sadly admits failures under some circumstances and blesses new attempts.

The wedding service itself moves guests as well as principals. They are reminded of the promises of their own wedding. Some of them have come to the church because the bride is their niece and politeness requires it, and they are surprised that ritualism brings back intentions that seemed past restoring. "There are a lot of things to be said about a wedding . . . a lot of thoughts that go on," Thornton Wilder writes in *Our Town*. Promise is the key thought; sacrament comes from the Latin *sacramentum*, the oath of allegiance that a Roman soldier took.

In marriage, the first pledge is by God to the bride and groom. If a wise old relative mutters under his breath, "God help the young fools," the answer is, "He will; we are here in church to add our prayers to His promise." The second oath of allegiance is taken by the bride and groom to each other. The minister says colloquially, "I married them," but when speaking carefully, he says, "I blessed their wedding; they married each other." His role is to solemnize matrimony.

Couples sometimes compose their own ritual, which is all right as long as the basic promises are included, for the bride and groom are the ones who celebrate the sacrament in which the clergyman assists. This procedure minimizes magic by making it clear to the bride and groom that they themselves are responsible for their marriage, God helping them. Christ is present whether or not they are aware of him, as Amos Niven Wilder describes in *A Runaway Marriage*:

Brother and sister in this world's poor family,
Jack and Jill out of this gypsy camp of an earth . . .

Come for his benediction whom they have blasphemed,
And somehow sense that they touch—what?
God, the Higher, all that they have missed:
Innocence and mercy and compassion . . .

No bridesmaids nor flowers for you,
The groom hasn't given you these.
You come in an old coat.
One of the gang is best man and witness.
The boy minister goes through with it,
And there is no shower as you go out . . .
It is movie night in the village, and no one is
    about to spy you at the parsonage,
And so you go off in the blizzard to the lumber camps.
This is all the world gives you.

But the Son of Man of the wedding feast haunts such
    occasions and understands you.

He can turn the water into wine and such shame and
  loss into gain
In some world some time.

Ordination

Like a wedding, the ordination of a clergyman is another
church ritual attended chiefly by friends and relatives. The
service itself is very ancient; its high point is the laying on
of hands by a bishop, other clergy, or both. In some
churches, a person is ordained simply by being given the
right hand of fellowship. Ordination makes him the spiritual leader of his church to carry out its work of ministry to people, to conduct its ritual, and to celebrate its
sacraments. He has many names: priest, minister, clergyman, rabbi, presbyter, pastor, father, preacher, parson,
chaplain, padre, cleric, and the colloquial "reverend."
These titles have different nuances, but beneath them all is
the same person: someone freed from other responsibilities
to tell people about God. Ordination sets him apart for this
very thing.

He may have the additional title of pope, cardinal,
metropolitan, archbishop, bishop, president, prelate, dean,
canon, secretary, rector, curate, vicar, moderator, cele-
brant, stated clerk, abbot, presiding bishop, district super-
intendent—all grades within the ordained ranks established for special functions. Sometimes these extra duties
are temporary, sometimes conferred for life by further
rites. "Monsignor" and "doctor in divinity" are honorary
titles that give pleasure to the recipient and still more pleasure to his friends. Notwithstanding what rank or academic
degree he holds, every clergyman thinks of himself primarily as a pastor, ordained to serve others for God. One of
the Pope's oldest titles is "Servant of the Servants of God."

When the idea of the ministry first crossed my mind, I

doubted whether such work could ever be full-time. Even supposing such intimations of God as I had were true, was it reasonable to spend a lifetime trying to communicate them to others? Isn't faith, after all, a matter of individual temperament, almost a built-in response that some people have and some don't? I was a graduate mechanical engineer, employed in building construction, knowing few humanists; my friends were engineers. The few clergy I knew fitted the stale description: invisible six days of the week and incomprehensible on the seventh. The churches I attended never had interesting preaching, so I never thought anyone was affected by it. Yet I quickly add that I am grateful to conforming parents who took me to religious services. Even dull ritualism may come alive and fill a God-shaped vacuum in a child's life.

My own doubts about the usefulness of the ministry occur occasionally to everyone attending church. How can the officiant justify taking time from the workaday world for this occupation? In the slang of another day, what's his excuse for living? I focused the question for myself by thinking of a shipwrecked company on a desert island. Some of the survivors would build shelters, some farm, some nurse, some cook; each would do what he could to help the community survive. Would anyone be excused from the daily chores for an intangible thing like religion? Could he be freed even part-time from running the laundry or catching fish? If he were, would he contribute anything to the struggle for existence?

I gradually learned that the answer is yes, although I didn't know it for certain until I became a candidate for ordination and went to the seminary. Then I was overwhelmed with the extent of people's hidden interest in God, and I began to realize the need for ministers. Laundering and fishing go better if there is a priest around. Every drama about a shipwreck island hangs on one castaway giving courage to the others. Television westerns always have persuaders; the good guys who talk to the bad guys. This need for spiritual leadership is plain in shipwrecks and in the old Wild West but is less clear in settled communities. Yet scholarly criminologists say that the absence of strong spiritual leadership may be the chief cause of the crime wave that threatens our communities. The criminologists are beginning to question the facile assumption of the past fifty years that crime is society's fault more than the perpetrator's. Recent studies are beginning to show that removing unemployment, poverty, poor education, slow justice, and bad prisons will not greatly reduce the number of criminals. Any of these things by itself or all together will not do as much as elevating men's motives would. What is needed is to strengthen those religious attitudes that are the powerful factor in conduct.

It must be explained all over again to each generation that certain acts are wrong whether or not one is caught. The sign displayed in city buses, "Shoplifting is dumb," is itself a dumb sign. "Shoplifting is a sin" would have been more fundamental, however pious it sounds, because it states the ultimate sanction for conduct. The commandment against stealing was one of the ten by which God brought man out of the jungle, and it still evokes an instinctive response in human nature. Al Smith, Felix Frankfurter, and Daniel Patrick Moynihan came out of the same city jungle that produced the "godfathers." The difference was in their homes, which had effective church or synagogue backing.

Editorials on "The Need for Morality" or "The Poor Must Become Future-Oriented" never go on to tell who will persuade people into these attitudes. The haunting background question is, Who brings about these changes? Who ties the bell on the cat? In my own life, I came only gradually to see that it is the man who speaks for God. This is not to say that the ordained person is the only one who ties bells; many others do also—the lawyer, artist, politician, labor leader, doctor, parent (supremely), and the person in the maligned communications media. But behind them all and constantly at it is the person society sets free to be pontifex, the maker of bridges from man to man and from man to God.

It is often said that Lincoln was the greatest theologian ever to occupy the White House. If this is so, it would be fair to add that it was mainly because of James Smith, a missionary from Scotland, who was minister of the Presbyterian Church in Springfield, Illinois. The Lincolns met Mr. Smith when their second son died. They sought him out because the Episcopal minister who had married them was out of town. Lincoln became a regular church attender and a lifelong friend of the minister's. He was deeply impressed with a scholarly defense of Christianity written by Smith. When Lincoln died, the family sent one of his gold-headed canes, as a token of their esteem and affection, to the missionary, then living in retirement in his native Dundee.

In the early days of World War II, when Poland was dismembered, whole village populations were transported to distant places. Often they were sent in unheated trains, without food or medical care. In such hardships, the people survived if there was someone in the company to tell about home, make jokes, or play the harmonica. By contrast, in trains with food and heat but no speech or music, the uprooted peasants sometimes died of broken hearts. The minister is the harmonica player. Lawyers incorporate railroads, bankers finance them, train crews run them, doctors mend bodies, and cooks prepare meals, but someone has to make music. Listen to irascible Thomas Carlyle a century ago:

> That a man stand there and speak of spiritual things to me, it is beautiful; even in its great obscurity and decadence it is among the beautifulest, most touching

objects one sees on this earth. This speaking man had indeed, in these times, wandered terribly from the point, yet at the bottom whom have we to compare with him? Of all such functionaries boarded and lodged on the industry of modern Europe, is there one worthier of the board he has? . . . The speaking function, with all our writing and printing function, has a perennial place, could he but find the point again.

Standing up in the exiles' train, or preaching, is never the minister's only work. His greatest contribution is friendship; he spends his full time doing what other men can only do part time. He may accomplish more by conversation than by sermon; he prepares people for the sacraments as much as he "dispenses" (unfortunate word) them. He not only works in the church building but also hangs around the general store for "contacts" (another unfortunate word). He talks to people before they marry, advises parents whose infants he has baptized, is an honorary uncle to children, and—at the last—comforts those who mourn. He visits constantly (*Jeremiah* 23:2).

A wise Roman Catholic archbishop said there were three rules for conversion: kindness, kindness, and kindness. "Who is weak, and I am not weak? Who is offended, and I burn not?" (*2 Corinthians* 11:29). The priest is one person who is not above any menial service, as shown by stories out of prisoner-of-war camps, another version of a shipwreck island. Back in civilization, he is on the committee if the community needs a library, a school, or a hospital. When the garbage is not collected in the slums, that's his job; just as explaining life's meaning to Falstaff's peppercorns and brewers' horses is his job in the neighborhoods where garbage collection is rarely neglected.

Parson is Old English for the *Person*, the friend-at-large, the last generalist in a world of specialists. The community recognizes his function and senses that God has chosen him for it. Even the fiercest republicans, who cannot conceive of God's Anointed King (*1 Samuel* 10:1), have respect for God's Anointed Prophet (*2 Kings* 2:15). They expect him to speak for God, no matter how stumbling his witness. They open themselves to him, and as a consequence he becomes a channel not only from heaven to earth but also from strong men to weak men. The ordained person teaches people and also learns from them; he is instructed and ennobled by laymen all his life. On the shipwreck island he may have been called to the ministry by the unordained: "Look, Joe, I'll lay your bricks for you if you'll knock off now and get up a church service for tomorrow."

If an agnostic has the fleeting idea that he ought to volunteer for ordination, it is not as preposterous as it seems at first. Sheep dogs don't come from sheep, they come from wolves. A Roman Catholic order was wise to advertise for candidates in an elite sex magazine. Since man does not live by bread alone, those who have found nothing but bread are most aware of their need for something more. Awareness of hunger in oneself is often God's call to the ministry. A man may not recognize his vocation at the time; later he remembers the conversations, the chance books, the opening of certain doors and the closing of others. Men miss their life work waiting for a heavenly sign, when the sign is the wistfulness they see in themselves and in their contemporaries. And it is apt to be accompanied by the misgivings of the Polish harmonica player. Who told *him* to stand up in the train and play? How does he know he will be any good at it? David's call was that no one else went out to fight Goliath, so David did.

The impulse to the ministry comes ultimately from God, but this view can hardly be mentioned to beginners, because it implies a certainty they do not have. It is only later that they see they did not choose; they were called. "Ye have not chosen me, but I have chosen you, and ordained you" (*John* 15:16). The best men hesitate to claim much assurance at the start. Even at their ordination, when they are asked, "Do you think that you are truly called to the Ministry?," they are expected to answer only,

"I trust so."

"I think so."

Healing of the Body

Healing of the body has always been one of the ritualisms of the Church. Yet a sick agnostic can be scared out of his wits if he's visited in the hospital by a clergyman; the patient thinks it means he is going to die. But the clergyman calls to help him get well, not to prepare him for death. By his presence in the sick room he is a reminder that God heals bodies. The priest may say a prayer or he may do nothing but pass the time of day, but whether his visit lasts half a minute or half an hour, its aim is to heal. No matter how busy with preaching and planning, "important committee after important committee," the clergyman always calls on the sick, or he telephones, or writes a card. This concern is more than a vestigial remainder of the ancient rite of healing. It has always been a central practice of the Church, one of the glories of primitive Christians and of the Jews before them. "Let him come now to me, and he shall know that there is a prophet in Israel," said Elisha, and Naaman the leper did come, and when he "dipped himself seven times in Jordan, according to the saying of the man of God . . . his flesh came again like unto the flesh of a little child, and he was clean" (*2 Kings* 5:14). When Jesus sent out his disciples, his orders were, "As ye go, preach, saying, The kingdom of heaven is at hand. Heal the sick, cleanse the lepers, raise the dead, cast out devils" (*Matthew* 10:7–8).

Anyone reading the Bible for the first time might think Jesus was a doctor more than a clergyman. Following his example, the early Church prayed for the sick, often laid hands on them, and sometimes anointed them with oil. This last rite was known as unction, and it continued to be observed for nearly eight hundred years of Christian history until it was narrowed down to anointing of the dying. It was then called extreme unction (unction *in extremis*), its purpose being not to increase life but to prepare for death. It continued this way in the Roman Catholic Church but was given up by the Protestant Church at the Reformation. In 1962, the Vatican II Council broke unction away from its exclusive connection with death by returning it to its original use for all healing.

The present revival of healing is the continuance of the old sacrament of unction, which has been practiced intermittently in all Christian churches. Its partial disuse came in the nineteenth century, when medicine began to make rapid progress and people assumed that their ancestors had prayed for the sick because they did not know what else to do. Some secularists even predicted that with continued medical advances, prayer would eventually be abandoned altogether. Sigmund Freud helped unsettle this extreme materialism by suggesting that the time will come when we may see that all physical ills are mental. His exaggeration was a way of saying that while physical medicine continues to gain ground, spiritual force always accompanies and reinforces it. Drugs and surgery go forward, but believers never stop praying. Their motto is: Man tends, God mends. The medieval practice of chaining the insane to the church altar was a pathetic and natural groping toward God's healing. Now the mentally ill are in hospitals. The combination of pills and prayers is called sacramental by religion, psychosomatic by medicine. Man is a body-soul or a soul-body, never a body or a soul; materialism alone and spiritualism alone are both wrong. The surgeon on my battleship in the Pacific used to grumble, "It's all in your head, boys," but he was free with his drugs and scalpel.

Divine healing never suggests that we should neglect human care. Once when I took the Holy Communion to an Asian friend who was critically ill, I found his hospital room filled with servants and relatives. As I entered, his wife pointed to certain ones and said, "Christian," and they dropped to their knees. "The rest are Buddhists," she said, "and do not want the Communion." After the service I touched the sick man in blessing; then I told his wife she must get the people out of the room because they were disturbing him. She objected. "In our country," she said, "we believe that friends should crowd a sick room to prevent evil spirits from getting in." I replied, "But we are Christians and do not believe any such nonsense. The crowd is bad; get them out!" I helped push them, and the doctor almost wept with relief since he had been trying to accomplish this result for days. Anyway, the patient got well, religion insisting on science.

The close connection of physical and spiritual healing was shown long before Christ by Greek medicine, which treated the whole man. Greek health resorts contained not only rooms for the sick but also theaters, sports stadia, beautiful scenery, and religious temples. Just so, Christian healing depends on medicine, reading, music, exercise, flowers, and prayer. It is a total treatment. There is more eating and drinking in the Bible than in all of Charles Dickens's work or in Ian Fleming's James Bond 007 series. "He put his hand to his mouth; and his eyes were enlightened" (*1 Samuel* 14:27) sounds disconnected, but it means he ate something and hence could think better. Five hundred years before Christ, when Greeks were dying of appendicitis, the people they were able to cure were helped by food and drugs as well as by incantations. And five hundred years from now, when cancer is banished and man lives to be ninety-nine, his bodily health will still depend on prayer as well as medicine.

Unction is for everyone; God strengthens the strong as

well as heals the weak. It was for this reason that Queen Elizabeth II was anointed with oil at her coronation in 1953. She was young and healthy with responsibilities to which she was humanly equal; the prayers in Westminster Abbey asked God to make her even more healthy. In the same way, more strength for the strong is the intention of the locker-room devotions of football teams. God brings courage into space ships as well as into hospital wards; more life to the lively and perfect freedom to those already free. A wise professor puzzled a college chaplain by asking him whether his ministry to students was "the sentimental approach." The professor explained, "Do you see only the homesick, the meatballs, the drunks and would-be suicides and neglect the garden variety of undergraduate who comes to church?" He might have used Shakespeare's symbolism: Do you concern yourself only with peppercorns and brewers' horses?

The cooperation of the patient is often needed but not (repeat *not*) always. Finally, it is God who heals, not faith, or prayer, or spiritual awareness; so divine healing is a better expression than faith healing. God answers prayer no matter how weak the one who prays or the one who is prayed for, but as their strength grows, so does their ability to receive from Him. To say, as the Church does, that a sacrament does not depend on personality is only a flat way of insisting that God acts beyond all human agents.

My first vivid awareness of healing of the body came one afternoon as a young clergyman at the bedside of a woman who at eighty-two had had an appendectomy. She was frail; I held her hand and prayed (perhaps because it was expected of me) something like, "O God, help dear Alice, strengthen her and make her feel Thy peace and power in her soul, through Jesus Christ our Lord." Her wasted body seemed to fill out at once, her spirits revived; she got better and we had several more years of playing bridge with her large cards (she was half blind). This I saw, and I did not expect to see it; I know she did not expect it. She used to tease me that she was an unbeliever, but the poor old thing was down, and I prayed before she could object, an instance of sacramental grace in spite of feeble officiant and participant. Of course, her recovery could have been a coincidence, but as Archbishop William Temple of Canterbury observed, "When I stop praying, I notice coincidences stop."

Years later, while I was away in the Navy, healing services were started in my parish by a small group that gathered twice a month on a weekday. I continued these meetings when I returned, mainly because it seemed a shame to stop any good thing (not a very positive motive). There were no dramatic scenes; some people were cured although not all; and there was a quiet confidence, which gradually spread to me. Quietness may be the essential note for Christian healing, as it was in Bible times: "Tell no man; but go thy way, show thyself to the priest" (*Matthew* 8:4). Another Archbishop of Canterbury, Michael Ramsey, said, "The note of restraint is all-important—that shrinking from the spectacular." In my congregation, most of the members paid no attention to the healing services (I never preached about them at a Sunday service), but they never questioned them, because the practice is Biblical and is provided for in our *Book of Common Prayer* by a ritual with a form of words:

I anoint thee with oil (*or* I lay my hand upon thee), In the Name of the Father, and of the Son, and of the Holy Ghost; beseeching the mercy of our Lord Jesus Christ, that all thy pain and sickness of body being put to flight, the blessing of health may be restored unto thee. Amen.

Such practices can go unused for hundreds of years but are never lost, because they are bound in a printed book:

another advantage of an established ritual. Following the prayers for healing, there comes an apparently inconsistent note:

> The Minister is ordered, from time to time, to advise the People, whilst they are in health, to make wills arranging for the disposal of their temporal goods, and, when of ability, to leave Bequests for religious and charitable uses.

Here is no nonsense about sickness and death being errors that man will ultimately banish. The plain idea is, let us be healthy while we are alive; let us open our bodies both to medicine and to God's spirit. And also make our wills.

Two

MYSTICISM

Being Drawn Toward God

Is this book saying that anyone who wants to find out what comes after bread might start attending weddings, ordinations, and the like? Yes, that is what I meant by the abrupt CHURCH on the post card to the psychoanalyst. It was shorthand for what is spelled out on a brass plate in Christ Church, Cambridge, Massachusetts: "Seated in this pew, 1876–1928, Sturgis Hooper Thorndike first was drawn towards loyalty to God and to God's cosmos." A Harvard professor wrote that tablet fifty years ago, and in that church every Sunday since before the American Revolution, individuals seated here and there in the congregation have been drawn toward God.

It happens in every church; its technical name is mysticism. Ritualism (not forgetting the inside of a church) opens to mysticism (being drawn toward God). As ritualism conveys a good and a bad taste, so does mysticism. I'll try to separate the good and bad in mysticism before going on to the remaining church rites.

The bad is what communications engineers refer to as "noise in the information system." For instance, the "noise" you have to remove is the notion that *information about God* is the same thing as God. Information might lead to God as a road map can guide a driver, or a musical score a pianist, but the piece of paper is not the land or the music. This is why the psychoanalyst seized so quickly on my suggestion of "information" as a substitute for "every word that proceedeth out of the mouth of the Lord," the Hebrew poet's phrase for the Very Presence of God. The psychoanalyst was no religious illiterate; his reference to the *Saint James Version* was only a slip of the tongue. His glee at catching me out on an elementary distinction was evident in the casualness of the question on his post card: "By the way, what is the information?" He thought faster than I did and knew that information by itself can be sterile.

> God guard me from those thoughts men think
> In the mind alone;
> He that sings a lasting song
> Thinks in a marrow-bone.

> I pray (for fashion's word is out
> And prayer comes round again)
> That I may seem, though I die old,
> A foolish, passionate man.

> —*W. B. Yeats*

Mysticism from a Magazine

Thinking in a marrow bone is illustrated in the life of Albert Schweitzer, one of the heroes of the twentieth century. In 1965, when he died at the age of ninety, he was a famous medical missionary, theologian, and musician. In 1906, as a young pastor in Alsace, he had written *The Quest of the Historical Jesus*, a book addressed to theologians. It was a scholarly analysis of the impossibility of knowing the historical Jesus "in depth," as the current idiom would put it. Yet the book ended with this paragraph, which seemed to contradict the whole thesis:

He comes to us as One unknown, without a name, as of old, by the lakeside, He came to those men who knew Him not. He speaks to us the same word: "Follow thou me!" and sets us to the tasks which He has to fulfill for our time. He commands. And to those who obey Him, whether they be wise or simple, He will reveal Himself in the toils, the conflicts, the sufferings which they shall pass through in His fellowship, and, as an ineffable mystery, they shall learn in their own experience Who He is.

Describing such a confrontation was no conventional piety with Schweitzer, as all the world knows. At the time he was writing his book, he decided to give up careers in theology and music, two fields in which he was a giant, and study medicine to go to Africa as a doctor. Although he was needed in civilization as a pastor, scholar, and organist, he chose to be a missionary in the jungle. His friends thought he was not quite right in his head and treated him with affectionate mockery.

He said he did it for two reasons: first, because reading the Bible made him see Africa as Lazarus, the beggar, laid at the gate of the rich man, Europe (*Luke* 16:19–31). And second, because one evening he found a magazine of the Paris Missionary Society, which had been laid on his writing table during his absence. In the very act of putting it aside so he could go on with his work, he mechanically opened it and read an appeal that expressed the hope it would bring some of those "on whom the Master's eyes already rested" to a decision to offer themselves for the Congo Mission. "Men and women who can reply simply to the Master's call, 'Lord, I am coming,' those are the people whom the Church needs." Schweitzer concludes, "The article finished, I quietly began my work. My search was over."

The Bible is man's guide for conduct, but in spite of loud information noise to the contrary, it is not his sole guide.

To it must be added today's direction from the living Holy Spirit. The book cannot be used as a Do-It-Yourself manual; it must be supplemented by new light directly from God as new situations arise. Jesus said, "I have yet many things to say unto you, but ye cannot bear them now. Howbeit when he, the Spirit of truth is come, he will guide you into all truth" (*John* 16:12–13).

Most important, this direct guidance from God is the experience of common people. In the Bible the Spirit comes on ordinary occasions in contrast to pagan writings which limit Him to the extraordinary. The non-Bible mentality looks for the supernatural in the unnatural. Because sneezing was incomprehensible to primitive man, he thought it was an intrusion of the divine and that is why we still say, "God bless you!" when someone sneezes. Ignorance of the relation between intercourse and offspring made the cave man regard a baby as a visitation from the spirit world. So a woman was taboo for weeks after childbirth. Death also appeared as an inexplicable mystery; consequently the aborigine held dead bodies in awe. Primitive bewilderment at the enigmas of sneezing, birth, and death survive in a few Bible passages that cite them as evidence of God's presence, but the book's overwhelming testimony is the other way—that the supernatural is to be found in the natural. The typical Judeo-Christian conviction is: "So is the kingdom of God, as if a man should cast seed into the ground . . . and the seed should spring and grow up, he knoweth not how. For the earth bringeth forth fruit of herself; first the blade, then the ear, after that the full corn in the ear" (*Mark* 4:26–28). In the Bible the Spirit comes routinely, felt by everyday persons who are quite different from the eccentrics sometimes listed in the appendixes of textbooks. "There is that of God in every man" is the only dogma of the undogmatic Quakers.

"Mysticism is by no means confined to a few chosen spirits and rare geniuses," wrote Quaker Rufus Jones. "It is a widespread fact to be reckoned with everywhere—this immediate correspondence with Someone, a Holy Spirit, a Great Companion—this *furtherance of life* by incoming energy, the heightening of power by correspondence with what *seems* to be God." He used to say with a Maine accent that he was a mystic (a fighting word in the 1930s), his big farmer's hands folded across his chest, his blue eyes taking in everything through rimless glasses. He was an administrator of large relief funds as well as a scholar, a striking illustration of the matter-of-factness of the presence of God.

> The world is charged with the grandeur of God.
> It will flame out, like shining from shook foil.
> —*Gerard Manley Hopkins*

It is almost necessary to be a parish minister to realize how many average people see this shining from shook foil. They are so normal that their mystical life goes unobserved. "You make me uneasy when you talk about your voices," the Bastard of Orleans says to Joan of Arc in Shaw's *Saint Joan*. "I should think you were a bit cracked if I hadn't noticed that you give me very sensible reasons for what you do." Joan, who in Shaw's play and in real life, was an earthy peasant girl, replies, "Well, I have to find reasons for you because you do not believe in my voices. But the voices come first; and I find the reasons after; whatever you may choose to believe."

When I hear someone say that God told him to do a certain thing, the hair stands up on my neck. But before I believe him, I have to be sure he has common sense and knows the Bible. An instance of common sense is Albert Schweitzer's attitude toward two invitations. He refused an honorary degree at the three hundredth anniversary of Harvard University, probably the only one of the invited fifty who did. His grounds were that he could not leave his work in Africa. A few years later, he was invited to Aspen, Colorado, to give a lecture. Again he declined until Thornton Wilder, who was on the committee, whispered, "Money!" So they offered Dr. Schweitzer $3,000 for his hospital, a significant sum at that time. He accepted and came to Aspen to lecture on Goethe. Perhaps this seems like uncommon sense, to prefer $3,000 worth of medicine to an honorary degree. In any event, commonplaceness is one of the marks of God's Spirit.

Humdrum mysticism is also illustrated by an entry in Henry Thoreau's *Journal* about being seasick on the rough ocean off the coast of Massachusetts: "Midnight—head over the boat's side—between sleeping and waking—with glimpses of one or more lights in the vicinity of Cape Ann. Bright moonlight—the effect heightened by seasickness." Someone has said that in Thoreau the natural scene was heightened, not depressed, by a disturbance of the stomach, and nausea met its match at last. This steadiness is at the heart of *Walden*—undeviating gratitude for the life-everlasting that he found growing in his own back yard.

Every Man His Own Epistemologist

How real is this life-everlasting found growing in anyone's own back yard? The question is sharpened by the story of an artist brought up in Aix-en-Provence. In his youth it was the custom for families to send flowers at New Year's to any house where they had dined in the course of the year. His family had a friend named Paul Cézanne who did a strange thing: he sent paintings of flowers instead of real bouquets. These gifts became embarrassing. Mother wouldn't put them in the attic, because it was already cluttered with Cousin Mathilde's bedstead; Father wouldn't have them in the cellar, because he was afraid the fresh paint might spoil the wine. So they were hung in odd places around the house until Cézanne moved away. Then the family decided to get rid of the paintings by burning them. But it is not polite to burn a friend's paintings in front of the servants. But the servants were off on Sunday afternoons! So the old artist, who told the story to Thornton Wilder, often recalls with a shudder the Sunday as a child when he helped burn eleven major Cézannes in his own back yard.

How could such a thing happen? Is there anything real about beauty? Cézanne's paintings were worth almost nothing until late in his life. Earlier they were left by the side of the road and farmers used them to repair holes in chicken coops. After his death, they were cleaned of chicken droppings, bought by museums, and fought over in auctions. Is any judgment final in aesthetics? Or in any of the experiences sometimes denigrated as subjective—abstract thinking, conscience, love, and the sense of God? How do we know what we know?

The technical word for this study is epistemology, a name I never understood until I heard a professor playfully refer to "that small portion of my audience who are not trained epistemologists." Now I use the word all the time, partly for name dropping, but mostly because everyone is an epistemologist, trained or untrained. The methods anybody uses to get at facts are epistemological, even though he never heard the word.

One method is by measuring; it tells sure facts: this stone weighs more than that one, this field has more trees than yonder field. From time to time, someone will try to disturb us by insisting that only such mathematical data have value. It's an old point of view that generations of thoughtful adolescents keep rediscovering: "All we can be certain of," they say to their pained parents, "is what our five senses tell us—what we can taste, touch, smell, hear, or see. There's nothing else." At such a moment, Father wishes he were a trained epistemologist and Mother wishes she had kept the children more faithful to Sunday school. They may remember a quotation from Edward Caird, William Temple's teacher: "Number tells us something about everything, but very little about anything."

When the family stops trying to score points in every round, parents have to admit that reliance on the senses has brought the world fantastic blessings. This reliance is the scientific method that has advanced medicine and reduced poverty, to mention only two things. When the human race learned to count, it opened a cornucopia of good, for man is underdeveloped in just those places where he has failed to measure. The parent who knows his Bible will add that the scientific method is rooted in that book. It is no coincidence that the scientific world is the Western world is the Bible world. The Declaration of Independence first said, "We hold these truths to be sacred and undeniable," but the phrase was considered too pious and was changed to "We hold these truths to be self-evident." *Self-evident* is just as pious as *sacred* and *undeniable*. William Temple said that if God is not revealed in the rising of the sun every morning He cannot be revealed in the rising of the Son of man from the dead. Biblical epistemology is, "Prove all things; hold fast that which is good" (*1 Thessalonians* 5:21).

"Prove" brings the dialogue back into the boxing ring. The children reiterate that you cannot prove anything except what you can measure. Of course, instead of children, the skeptics might be two old aunts at Christmas dinner. The difference between children and their aunts, between young and old, is not that one is atheistic and the other theistic. "Generation gap" is only shorthand for saying that people of different years have different knowledge of the world and sometimes, but not always, find difficulty in communicating. The gap does not mean that the aged are always trying to convert youth to belief; some of the old are trying to convert the young to unbelief. Who has the statistics? "What young d'ya know?" or, "What old d'ya know?"

Whether young or old, the believers turn to definitions: "Suppose we don't say *prove*, but instead say *know*, *feel*, *sense*, or *perceive*. Are you saying that we have no impressions of anything except what we can touch, taste, smell, hear, or see? How do you explain that a painting is visible, although the fact of appreciating it is invisible? Because beauty is appreciated inside the mind and cannot be measured with a yardstick, do you imply it is not there? Do you say Cézanne's paintings have no value except the number of square feet of canvas available for a chicken coop?"

What this speech is getting at, whether addressed to children or their aunts, is that physical measurements are not the only ways to knowledge. "There are delights here not known by your Senses Five," said William Blake. Like beauty, goodness is an input to consciousness which some "see" and some do not. In the same way, heroism inspires one person and not another. Abstract reasoning is a further reality that has nothing to do with physical measurements: witness Albert Einstein making his discoveries by sitting in a chair with a yellow pad on his lap. God is felt by some people and not by others, altogether apart from material evidence. If He does not exist because He gives no touch, sight, sound, taste, or smell, neither do beauty or courage. If mysticism isn't valid, neither is an El Greco painting or the Congressional Medal of Honor.

On this subject, forty years ago, James Thurber drew a cartoon of a man sitting by himself at a party with his head on his fist, like Rodin's *Thinker*. One guest pointing to the solitary brooder says to another, "He doesn't know anything except facts!" The humor is that everyone believes he is in possession of nothing but facts. The question is, what are the facts? Thurber's joke was epistemology rearing its ugly head in a humorous magazine. The drawing caught the fancy of Robert Maynard Hutchins, at that time the youthful president of the University of Chicago. He wired Thurber asking if he would sell the original to him. Thurber wired back that he would send it to him as a gift. Dr. Hutchins used to say that he was more pleased with Thurber's drawing than with the millions from a foundation that arrived that same day for his university.

The cartoon was pinpointing the philosophy of education Chicago stood for in those days: that facts were not limited to science. Again, Blake's "There are delights here not known by your Senses Five." The hundred best books sponsored by Chicago was another way of making this point, since they obviously are not all mathematical treatises. They have been studied in colleges and informal groups ever since and are brought to the attention of visitors like Gertrude Stein in America on a lecture tour. She happened to sit next to one of Dr. Hutchins's assistants and asked him at dinner, "What do you do?" He told her he was promoting the hundred best books. "What are they?" she exclaimed in mock surprise. He always had the list with him, so he took it out of his pocket and she studied it. "There are a number of translations here," said Miss Stein in a dubious tone. "Of course," said the academician inadvertently arguing against his own best books. "This is a study of facts, not of aesthetics."

"There is no such thing as facts; there is only good writing," she replied, whether seriously or not is hard to tell.

"On the contrary, Miss Stein, there is more on one page of Adam Smith's *Wealth of Nations* than in all of Milton's *Paradise Lost*. Statistics tell more than poetry."

"Nonsense, young man," she replied, thrusting the list back at him. "There is more on one page of *Paradise Lost* than in all of the *Wealth of Nations*!"

Both were on the same side but probably only she knew it: the side that insists that facts come from other things than measuring. Milton's thoughts "Of Man's First Disobedience and the Fruit of that Forbidden Tree" give as many facts to live by as Smith's economic tabulations.

Besides, if tabulating is the only way to know anything, much that comes into the mind is unimportant to us. Few people care how many trees are in yonder field. Maybe they should be made to count them for the advancement of science, but at the same time they should be allowed to enjoy their beauty. They should not be battered by the tiresome chorus, "Only Math Matters." Some of my best friends are mathematicians who don't act on their own theory that there is nothing beyond calculus. They love their families, play the piano, go to art galleries, attend church at least while the children are young, and enlist in wartime when over age. It is their private conceit that they know nothing but facts, but that is the general assumption of everyone who reasons. The question is, do facts come from measuring only? Or do they also come from other methods of comprehending?

Mankind has always voted for this second possibility, that other methods exist in addition to the use of pocket calculators and the like. It has proclaimed this insight over the ages by referring to conscience, heart, will, feeling, and spirit as if they were separate bodily organs designed to take in separate kinds of information. The ancient theory was that different parts of the body grasped different aspects of reality. For instance, the soul alone knew God; early autopsies used to probe around to find it. The cave man's stomach was thought to absorb courage from eating lions' livers; bowels "yearn" in the Bible. Khrushchev's farewell to America was, "You have won my heart but not my head." Such constant references through history to various intake organs testify that the human race thinks the sensations taken in are of various kinds. Each is distinctive or separate, a quality covered by the word discrete. Thinking accurately is not caring for friends; one is truth, the other love. Spiritual awareness is not always tied to good conduct; one is mysticism, the other morality.

We no longer believe that there are separate organs for registering separate experiences. At last we have caught up with the Greek physician Hippocrates, author of the physicians' oath, who wrote about 400 B.C. against the theory of his day: "From the brain, and from the brain only arise our pleasures, joys, laughter and jests, as well as our sorrows, pains, griefs and tears." Even though there come into this single brain different types of information, they are not interchangeable. Mysticism, thinking, beauty, morals, and love are discrete facts of the real world, no one of which is reducible to any of the others. This view holds in spite of those who insist that beauty is truth and truth beauty, or that love is the only reality, or mysticism the totality of human experience. Such reductionism is the most common epistemological error.

We understand better *how we know what we know* at just this point—when we grasp that each of the varied impressions coming into the brain is a valid one. We must not let a materialistic magician razzle-dazzle us with colored lights, a raw egg, and a bowl of goldfish and pull out of a hat a single rabbit: "Only counting is valid." An attack on the reality of God because He cannot be weighed is an attack on most experience, because weighing is only a *section* of reality—the scientific one. It is a very important section and has brought untold blessings. But science will never include everything, contrary to the prediction that someday Beethoven's Fifth Symphony will be put into an equation and it won't be necessary to listen to the music.

What Do Drugs and Electrodes Tell Us?

If every man is his own epistemologist, sooner or later he has to decide what can be known by the new potentialities of drugs and electrodes. American prisoners in Asia were supposed to have been brainwashed by powders in their cereal, and the players in an international chess match in Iceland were reported to have been influenced by hidden electronics. The willingness to credit such tales comes from the proven results in many experiments, such as putting tiny electric wires in cats' brains to make them afraid of mice, so the cats run away from the mice. Shifting the electrode to another area of the cat's brain will make him brave enough to attack a wolf. From such operations it is inferred that brains can be deceived on anything, or can be as soon as science discovers which device to use. Certain drugs reach the area of the brain related to religion and seem to produce a mood remarkably like "joy and peace in believing" (*Romans* 15:13). So when someone hears that Christ will give him steadiness, he might ask whether this is the same as a tranquilizer.

At times, the potential of pills and wires seems so limitless that communities are proposed where life will be passed in a series of agreeable sensations physically induced in the neurocerebral system. Advocates of such escapism go on to hint that science will discover that God is a tiny electrical impulse, that honesty is a chemical, and friendliness a medication. Why can't a virus give us algebra as well as flu? A future is promised with electrodes in the brain spurring good thoughts and bypassing bad ones. Twenty-first-century man, under his hat, may look like the back of a television set. Such facetiousness is not meant to make fun of scientific research in this field but to urge that it go hand in hand with epistemology, which evaluates final results. "Science," wrote Oliver Wendell Holmes, "is the upstairs furnishings of the house which must be furnished downstairs with common sense."

Applying common sense to drugs, physicians report that their continued use can have disastrous side effects that lead to disintegration of personality and chromosome distortions. The body develops a tolerance so that more and more stimulation is needed; the mounting demand becomes insatiable and the victim is "hooked." On a different level, there exists among Navajo Indians what sociologists call the Peyote Cult, known officially as the Native American Church. It observes an all-night ritual with borrowings of Masonic ceremonial and church liturgy. Its unique feature is a small bean chewed by the worshiper to induce a mystical drowsiness. Whether it is habit-forming or brain-damaging is the subject of lawsuits and medical research. One immediate misgiving is whether the resulting exhilaration these Indians experience isn't the same thing Christians find in their worship. What is the difference between their bean and our God? Or more exactly, between a drug-induced happy state and a God-induced happy state? It may be shown that the bean heightens the same part of consciousness that God activates, but common sense maintains that activating only the mystical part of consciousness is not mature religion. God enters all of human life.

Some of the flower children who claimed to copy the Navajo cult by their Timothy Leary drugs showed no more of the characteristics of highly developed religion than the Navajos did. They had little logical thinking, no consistency in ethics, a heavy reliance on beads for beauty, and a moody amiability in place of their much advertised love. Before they can be accepted as valid prophets of a new reality, both the Native American Church and the drug culture will have to show long-range results in character and life style, not temporary sensations. The repugnance that many people feel for mystical "highs" comes from their awareness that such religion does not wear well. If, over the years, a faith produces strong and cheerful living, fine; if not, why bother? The same is true with drugs.

What is done today by drugs and electrodes was done long ago by crude medications. Parents trying to protect today's child from psychedelic experimentations are reenacting their grandparents' efforts to keep a child (or those same two old aunts) away from intoxicating patent medicines. When it is argued that drugs are no worse than alcohol and hence should be legalized, every doctor and priest winces. Alcohol has always been dangerous for many people; habitual drunkenness is appalling. Pious feelings may be evoked by wires in the head or aspirin taken with coffee, but solid consequences do not follow. LSD visions and artists' visions are not the same in the long run. Those who have "gone sciency" may refuse to recognize these difrences, but common sense insists they exist. John Yeats, the painter, father of the poet W. B. Yeats, observed once · that "science without philosophy is the opiate of the suburbs."

An artificial stimulation is never a substitute for the real thing. One day while pressing a button to induce sex feelings in a male rat, the experimenter remarked, "Of course, this doesn't do away with female rats." The wisecrack puts the matter into perspective. Of course (that wonderful putdown), tranquilizers do not replace serenity; of course, gin ("Dutch courage") is no substitute for bravery; and, of course, a high caused by a drug does not represent God's presence and His very Self.

Immature Forms of Mysticism

Even without drugs, it has always been known that fasting and sleeplessness can confuse brain functions, and immature religions settle for that, claiming to break through to reality by bodily dysfunctioning. It is the pagan tendency, already noted, to look for the supernatural in the unnatural.

In sharp contrast, the Bible advocates the clear-eyed observation that comes from food and rest. Jesus made his followers pause, no matter how busy: "Come ye yourselves apart into a desert place, and rest a while: for there were many coming and going, and they had no leisure so much as to eat" (*Mark* 6:31). God tells Elijah to eat, drink, and sleep before He speaks to him (*1 Kings* 19). And then He does not overwhelm the prophet by wind, earthquake, or fire but talks in a still, small voice. "Religious" sensations can come from frightening phenomena, but religious results come from quietness in a fed and rested person. True, the saints and martyrs were not always fed and rested, but neither did most of them deliberately seek suffering.

Superstition is another form of mysticism, sometimes harmless, persisting among those who throw spilled salt over their shoulder, knock on wood (increasingly difficult in a world of plastics), carry a rabbit's foot, and refuse to number a floor in a building the 13th. A Soviet magazine had a cartoon of an audience watching a movie, "The Fight Against Superstition—A People's Science Film." The overflow crowd is standing up, yet seat No. 13 is vacant in every row. These are mystical intuitions but are so crude they amount to magic. Their believers think they can coerce the spirit by certain numbers and actions, as construction workers banish bad luck by "topping out" a building when they have completed their steel skeleton. This is a rite passed down for a thousand years before there was any steel. The workers raise to the highest point of the construction a basket containing a flag, three handkerchiefs, a fir tree, corn, ribbons, eggs, flowers, a pair of handcuffs, and a jar of chicken blood. The teaching of astrology that the stars inexorably control our actions makes it important to know what heavenly sign we were born under. *Time* magazine reported that in 1965 France spent a billion dollars annually (more than it spends on scientific research) on an odd-lot collection of fortunetellers and clairvoyants. In Paris alone, there is one magic worker for every 120 Parisians compared with one doctor for every 514 citizens and one priest for every 5,000.

In addition to such half-innocent superstitions, there is a

mysticism that is harmful because it makes religious people do unethical things. The daily news furnishes puzzling instances. Some of its unfortunate victims have malfunctioning brains, so their lack of morals brings no blame on themselves or their mysticism, but others, apparently sane, give religion a bad name by failing to connect it with behavior. There are even deliberate disconnections made by such things as Satan worship, witches' covens, and so-called black masses. Such mysticism is not immature but unmoral and deliberately perverse.

The misuse of mysticism that has persisted over the ages is summed up by John Greenleaf Whittier's "The Brewing of Soma." Soma is an ancient East Indian drug that produced "a winged and glorious birth," and corresponds to what is known today as "getting high." The poem is a recital of mankind's mistaken efforts over the ages to induce mystical sensations not only by drugs but also by self-hypnotism. It ends with what has become a hymn:

> As in that child-world's early year,
>   Each after age has striven
> By music, incense, vigils drear,
> And trance, to bring the skies more near,
>   Or lift men up to heaven!
>
> Some fever of the blood and brain,
>   Some self-exalting spell,
> The scourger's keen delight of pain,
> The Dervish dance, the Orphic strain,
>   The wild-haired Bacchant's yell.
>
> And yet the past comes round again,
>   And new doth old fulfil;
> In sensual transports wild as vain
> We brew in many a Christian fane
>   The heathen Soma still!

Dear Lord and Father of mankind
Forgive our foolish ways!
Reclothe us in our rightful mind,
In purer lives thy service find,
In deeper rev'rence praise.

Breathe through the heats of our desire
Thy coolness and thy balm;
Let sense be dumb, let flesh retire;
Speak through the earthquake, wind, and fire,
O still, small voice of calm.

Pentecostalism

Pentecostalism is a demonstrative expression of mysticism. Its organized churches have a variety of names and practices. They and the "main line" churches that have occasional pentecostal meetings are known as spirit-filled, or charismatic (from the Greek for "gift of grace"). The person who can keep Methodists, Roman Catholics, and Lutherans clear in his mind is often confused by the spectrum of names under which pentecostalism appears. The general characteristics of the movement are outward manifestations that are believed to prove that the inner light truly comes from God. These signs are often distasteful to the general public and even to conventional Christians, yet most of them go back a long way in the Judeo-Christian tradition. When we first see the prophets of the Old Testament, they are God-intoxicated holy men, more like Islamic whirling dervishes than economic and political forecasters. The proverb in ancient Israel "Is Saul also among the prophets?" (*1 Samuel* 10:11) meant that the people questioned the king's part in ecstatic ritualisms. Later when "David danced before the Lord with all his might," his wife Michal "despised him in her heart" (*2 Samuel* 6:14–16). *The Acts of the Apostles* and the letters of the New Testament show an occasional exuberance in worship that was commended by some leaders and questioned by others.

To this day, thoughtful churchmen often are puzzled about pentecostalism. They wonder about the periodic outbursts of zeal, which long ago were driven underground or gradually became part of the Church's quieter life. They ask, weren't all these in fact forms of pentecostalism in their day—the early Franciscans, Waldensians, Albigensians, Hussites, Lollards, Quakers, Wesleyans, and Anabaptists?

Popular opinion assumes that after a while the establishment manages to throttle the newborn life in the Spirit and make it conform to pedestrian custom. But all generalities need scrutiny, and this one about an always reluctant hierarchy must be modified by remembering that church authorities by themselves could not dampen the fresh fire if the ordinary believer did not half dislike it. The lukewarm are made uncomfortable in their tepid faith by the newly enthusiastic. It was not only the Jewish and Roman authorities who crucified Christ, but the half-love, half-hate of the average citizen of Jerusalem. "Must then a Christ perish in torment in every age to save those that have no imagination?" asks Bernard Shaw in *Saint Joan* after her burning at the stake. Thus the thoughtful believer approaches pentecostal practices without scorn because he remembers they are present in the Bible and all history and their condemnation has never been unanimous. He is apt to lean toward the words of a quiet Quaker, Geoffrey Nuttal: "Better fanatic folkes than to lie cold and unmoved in starched propriety."

One special mark of pentecostalism since New Testament days has been speaking in tongues (glossolalia). The word comes from two Greek words that mean "uttering incoherent sounds to express joy in the Spirit," or they may mean "speaking in a real language the speaker has never studied and yet in which he is temporarily fluent." This second meaning requires further documentation and may have a relation to extrasensory perception (ESP).

Other marks of the spirit-filled are rhythmic handclapping, dancing, jumping, and encouraging the speaker with shouts. Uncontrolled shaking in their rites gave the Shakers of early America their name. Four hundred years ago, the Religious Society of Friends acquired their now dignified nickname, Quakers, because they quaked with enthusiasm in their meetings. These phenomena are inarticulate expressions of faith, and for that reason are distasteful to many. Yet, surprisingly, they may be good just because they are inarticulate. Demonstrations of the faith cannot be left to preachers, scholars, and others professional in the shaping of words. In the long history of religion, what appear at times to be lowbrow forms of demonstrating conviction are valuable because they have had a democratizing effect. It is one way in which "the last shall be first" (*Matthew* 19:30), says Dean Krister Stendahl of the Harvard Divinity School.

That pentecostalism has any bad associations at all is puzzling, because the name is derived from the Day of Pentecost, when the Spirit came to the first Christians, a day so important in Christian history that it is called the birthday of the Church, and with Christmas and Easter it is one of the three great Holy Days of the Christian year. Yet pentecostalism suffers overtones as derogatory as "nationalism" does in connection with the Fourth of July. The original event is told in the second chapter of *Acts:*

And when the day of Pentecost was fully come, they were all with one accord in one place. And suddenly there came a sound from heaven as of a rushing mighty wind, and it filled all the house where they were sitting. And there appeared unto them cloven

tongues like as of fire, and it sat upon each of them.
And they were all filled with the Holy Ghost, and
began to speak with other tongues, as the Spirit gave
them utterance. And there were dwelling at Jerusalem
Jews, devout men, out of every nation under heaven.
. . . And they were all amazed, and were in doubt,
saying one to another, What meaneth this? Others
mocking said, These men are full of new wine.

The day of Pentecost was originally a Jewish Holy Day
that celebrated the giving of the Ten Commandments on
Mount Sinai fifty days after the Passover escape from Egypt.
Pentecost means the fiftieth day, when a yearly remembrance
was held in the synagogues. So the preacher cannot resist
pointing out that the Spirit came to the first Christians,
who were all Jews, while they were routinely attending the
synagogue. Sturgis Hooper Thorndike was drawn toward
loyalty to God while he was routinely attending church,
1876–1928, in Cambridge, Massachusetts. At Pentecost,
the early Jewish Christians were keeping the annual Ten
Commandments Day. Perhaps Someone was trying to tell
them something by sending the Spirit on the anniversary of
the Commandments. Obedience to moral law was, after all,
the particular emphasis of the highly developed religion
the Christians inherited from the Jews. Judaism insisted
that the Creator is holy and desires virtue above ritualism,
or churchgoing: "I hate, I despise your feast days, and I
will not smell in your solemn assemblies. Though ye offer
me burnt offerings . . . I will not accept them. . . . But let
judgment run down as waters, and righteousness as a
mighty stream" (*Amos* 5:21–24).
The basic effect of Pentecost was power from God,
which is fundamental to all religion; there is no such thing
as religion without it. Yet by itself this power is only part of
Christianity; mysticism, if it is to be Christian, must be
accompanied by an effort to copy the example of Jesus.

At Bat with Three-and-Two

In the true mysticism I have been attempting to describe, contemporary pentecostal Christians both fail and succeed.

1. Their first failing comes when, forgetting that Pentecost is Ten Commandments Day, they neglect their families and shirk their daily employment. A wife busy with revival meetings slights her children and cooks poor meals for her husband; a husband feels so secure in God's love (which is good) that he does not feed the computer carefully in his bank job (which is bad). Such un-Christian aspects at the fringes of pentecostalism may come from lack of judgment about priorities. Or they may come from sheer ignorance of the Bible: hating father or mother because Jesus orders it (*Matthew* 10:35), or handling serpents and drinking poisons as proof of God's protecting spirit (*Mark* 16:18). Such travesties would horrify mystics like Albert Schweitzer, Rufus Jones, and Joan of Arc and bewilder the cleaning woman who gives a good day's work for her wages, supports her blind nephew, and is into the church every time it's open.

2. A second failing of pentecostals is an inclination to make spiritual ecstasy a full-time occupation, thus copying Hindu-Buddhist withdrawal from the world. They somehow missed the often-told story of the monk in his cell blessed by an angelic vision. At the very moment of the vision there was a knock on the door from a needy person, and the monk with great reluctance left his cell to help the poor man. Later he hurried back fearful that the vision had gone. But the angel was still there and said, "If you had not gone to do your duty, I would have disappeared." The Mount of Transfiguration leads at once to the sick child in the valley (*Luke* 9:28–45).

Pentecostals neglecting obligations and pentecostals hungering only for rapture lack what the Bible calls sanctification. For that small proportion of my readers who are not familiar with this word, sanctification means "growth in character." It is what the Church does quietly and the Salvation Army does dramatically. When they convert a drunk, he stops drinking but may still go on beating his wife. Six months later he stops beating her but is still stealing from his employer. By the following year he stops stealing, all under the continuing influence of the Church or the Salvation Army. Sanctification is this gradual improvement of bad areas in life, the steady correction of inconsistencies after conversion. To be spirit-filled is only the first step in a pilgrim's progress.

In the baseball season I say to myself that pentecostalism is standing with three-and-two, the situation when the man at bat has a count of three balls and two strikes. It is always a tense moment in the game, because the next pitch is decisive. It could give the batter four balls and a free trip to first base, or three strikes—and he's out. Or the batter might hit a foul ball, or a fair ball and get on base or be put out. But every ball thrown by the pitcher at three-and-two is important. So pentecostalism stands today at a turning point, as it has often stood before in Christian history. Its next move will have broad consequences. It may start a rally in this inning that will lead to a wide renewal of faith, or it may strike out and not come to bat again for another half century.

If neglect of responsibilities and the full-time seeking of ecstasy are against pentecostalism, what are the three balls?

1. Pentecostalism in one form or another is found right now in many of the needy areas of the world, working among the drop-outs and alcoholics of our culture, supporting reform movements in Latin America, and evangelizing undergraduates on campuses that have become morally neutral. It is an influence sustaining faith in the Soviet masses deprived of their churches. A Kremlinologist re-

marked years ago that the Politburo disliked John D. Rockefeller, Jr., not because he was a capitalist but because he was a Baptist and supported spirit-filled missions in the Soviet Union. These far-flung enterprises include a variety of pentecostals working partly through the organized churches and partly outside them, a cross section of Roman Catholics and Protestants, quiet sacramentalists and wearers of "I love Jesus" T-shirts.

The drop-out and alcoholic correspond to Shakespeare's peppercorn and brewer's horse. Today's Falstaffs, cursed with futility and addiction, often find pentecostal faith the only thing able to help because it is so sharply God-centered, exactly "what the inside of a church is made of." It is what is meant by saying, "Let the church be the church," or, "We need the Gospel ministry," or "The Church's message is salvation." There are many ways of describing strong Christian mysticism.

2. A second ball in pentecostalism's favor is its frequent success with the quiet agnostic when he begins to wonder about faith. Everyone comes to the church three times in his life at least, and these occasions are not, as the flippant often say, his baptism, wedding, and funeral. He comes when he is hit by trouble and wonders if faith could help; when a friend is faced with disaster; and when someone he knows is seized by what the agnostic regards as a delusion called religion. The delusion may be doing good to its supposed victim or it may be doing harm, but in either case, it is a visible factor in his behavior. Anyone who has laid the egg of agnosticism hates to have it disturbed, and now it *is* disturbed. For the theory that "God" is unknowable is faced with evidence that "God" seems to be doing good or doing harm, and even the agnostic wishes to "God" (so to speak) that He would intervene in a tragedy.

In such crises, pentecostalism is often the cutting edge of a new insight. Its effect is as critical as every swing of the batter when he stands at three-and-two. Or it could be likened to the Marines in a touch-and-go military situation; or to the unglamorous Coast Guardsmen who know the rocks and surf better than do blue-water sailors. To change the figure again, pentecostalism is the high-voltage religion a businessman had in mind when he said, "Our son was into heavy stuff, and the Jesus Freaks saved him." On this subject Dean Stendahl writes:

> Flashlight-battery-voltage Christianity is certainly not strong enough for fighting the drug habit. And no religious tradition can renew itself without the infusion of raw and fresh primary religious experience. . . . We non-charismatics need to have charismatics among us in the church if the church is to receive and express the fullness of the Christian life. Thus *we* need *them.*

3. The third ball is the rarely noticed success of pentecostalism (again in all its variety) with many who never joined the movement but have been impressed by someone inside it, and for years will remember his cheerfulness and zeal. In this vicarious sense, many undemonstrative Christians have experienced pentecostal flame. Although they never became pentecostals themselves, it was the emotional faith of a friend seen long ago that led them finally to turn to the Church and whisper, "Mother!"

While recognizing these three contributions of contemporary pentecostalism, I maintain that the pentecostals need the quiet Christians. *They* need *us* as much as *we* need *them.* Their home is in the Church, the family of God, where their status as children does not depend on the intensity of their experiences. Stendahl concludes:

> There are times and seasons in the long life of a Christian . . . spectacular breakthroughs and . . . slow growth. . . . Understandably, those who have had

strong and beautiful experiences like to have them
continue. If that experience eventually does not come
quite as freshly and as strongly as it once did, then
comes the temptation to 'help the Spirit' a little, that
is, to cheat. Which creates feelings of guilt. To be sure,
the established churches need the refreshing influx of
new and wider ranges of charismatic experience, but
in the long perspective of spiritual growth the individual charismatic needs the home of the full church in
which he or she matures in faith and learns the most
important lesson of faith: to love God Who gave the
gift rather than to love the gift that God gave.

The demonstrative path and the quiet path are comple-
mentary ways by which people become aware of God. The
ignorant on both paths believe that only their way is truly
Christian, and they are both wrong. Each is fostering an
elitism that has a divisive effect in the churches, because
they do not take in what the Bible keeps repeating: "there
are diversities of gifts, but the same Spirit" (*1 Corinthians*
12:4). The outward expressions of pentecostalism, so dear
to television, are not proofs of God's Spirit. They may accompany the Spirit, but they are never the infallible evidences of His presence and might even be signs of the false
spirits, devils, and anti-Christ that the New Testament dis-
tinguishes from the true Spirit (*1 John* 4:1). Earlier the
Old Testament agonized over true and false spirits in the
prophets (*Jeremiah* 5:31). It is hard to say whether a so-
called evil spirit with a devastating influence is a living
adversary of God's, or whether it is some aberration of the
human mind. Does the phenomenon belong under theology
or psychology? But it is never hard to test God's Spirit by
the consequences. "The fruit of the Spirit is love, joy, peace,
longsuffering, gentleness, goodness, faith, meekness, temperance" (*Galatians* 5:22–23).

The Discipline of Christian Mysticism

Suppose we avoid pentecostalism when it is immature; disregard devil cults, silly superstitions, drugs, electrodes, and all forms of religious self-hypnotism, and look only at the highest communion with God. But this, too, presents intellectual difficulty. Stephen Vincent Benét describes Abraham Lincoln's dilemma:

> What is God's will?
> They come to me and talk about God's will
> In righteous deputations and platoons,
> Day after day, laymen and ministers,
> They write me Prayers from Twenty Million Souls
> Defining me God's will and Horace Greeley's. . . .
> It is the will of the Chicago churches,
> It is this man's and his worst enemy's.
> But all of them are sure they know God's will.
> I am the only man who does not know it.

Spiritual uncertainty did not discourage Abraham Lincoln, who said he "probably had to go on in a twilight, feeling and reasoning my way through life." To escape this twilight, the rationalist chooses noontime, when his eyes are dazzled by brightness, and the emotionalist chooses night when he can hardly see anything. The disciplined believer, on the other hand, walks between the two in a gray zone combining observation and intuition, his own intelligence, and God's voice. He is like his counterpart in science, described by Caryl P. Haskins as "the gifted unorthodox individual in the laboratory, or the study, or the walk by the river at twilight who has always brought to us all the basic resources by which we live." Religion and science alike share a light/dark quality described as enough light for those who wholly desire to see and enough obscurity for those who have a contrary disposition.

Lincoln's mysticism has this quality. His writing was ennobled by the English of the King James Version, but even more it was constantly corrected by the ideas that are the same in any version. Lincoln was a profound Christian thinker not only because he read the Bible all his life but also because he depended on the ongoing direction of the Spirit, the dual theme of Albert Schweitzer's 1906 *Quest*. Schweitzer's book astonished scholars by documenting that the Bible does not go into biographical details of Jesus's life. But even more astonishing was Schweitzer's closing paragraph about Jesus's presence now. "He comes to us as one unknown. . . . He commands. . . ."

Without the voice of the Spirit to give contemporary guidance, the Bible by itself is like the blueprint of an old building in which changes have been made. Its ambiguity about slavery was used to justify this institution before our Civil War. A letter called *Philemon*, written by Paul, returns a runaway slave to his master on the ground that a runaway is a thief who has stolen himself and now, having become a Christian, he must make restitution and give himself up. This New Testament book seems to have gone backward ethically from the Old Testament teaching in *Deuteronomy* 23:15: "Thou shalt not deliver unto his master the servant which is escaped from his master unto thee."

These apparent contradictions are called progressive revelation in religion, and mean that God progressively reveals more and more of His will to man, but also—and this is most important—that man grows in his understanding of what God has revealed. This concept of new truth applies in every other field as well as in religion and meets universal opposition. John Crosby, the columnist, once offered to write a television drama suitable for any new idea; all you need for suspense, he said, is someone to state the contrary opinion:

"Chris, give up this madness about discovering a New World."

"Damn it, Pasteur! What is this nonsense about germs?"

"Go back to sleep, Sigmund. Analyzing dreams will never get you anywhere."

Similar objections to new information abound in the Bible:

"Are not . . . rivers of Damascus, better than all the waters of Israel? may I not wash in them, and be clean?" (*2 Kings* 5:12).

"Be it far from thee, Lord: this shall not be unto thee" (*Matthew* 16:22).

"Not so, Lord; for I have never eaten any thing that is common" (*Acts* 10:14).

Against this attitude, Jesus said over and over, "It was said by them of old time . . . But I say unto you" (*Matthew* 5:21–22).

It is important to emphasize that the Holy Spirit is the agent of advance in all effort, not only in religion. He makes soldiers brave, violinists skillful, storekeepers scrupulous, and research scientists imaginative. The jingle we learned in our childhood about the Spirit is too limiting:

> He makes us go to Sunday school
> And all obey the Golden Rule.

"The farmer who cares for his land and neglects his prayers is, as a farmer, cooperating with God; and the farmer who says his prayers but neglects his land is failing, as a farmer, to cooperate with God," wrote William Temple. "It is a great mistake to suppose that God is only, or even chiefly, concerned with religion." The Roman Catholic Red Mass is not for the conversion of Reds, but to invoke the Holy Ghost (red altar hangings for fire and blood) in the administration of justice. It begs Him to convert the courthouse gang, if you like.

The Bible and the Spirit must be heeded together. Reliance on the Spirit alone, without continuous study of the Bible, can lead to undisciplined mysticism, as illustrated in two widely read novels. Boris Pasternak's *Dr. Zhivago* begins with a Christian funeral and employs the beautiful words of resurrection faith throughout the book, but the hero abandons his wife and children for a mistress and then in turn abandons her for another mistress. And though the revolutionary times cry out for doctors, he seldom practices his profession. Why, then, did the Soviet government ban the book when it might have used it effectively to ridicule the moral lapses of the religious? Because it took Zhivago to be the popular notion of a saint, undutiful, even unfaithful, but withal strong in mysticism. The Kremlin suppressed the book lest it strengthen ignorant belief and inspire churchgoing.

The other novel is *Heaven's My Destination*, in which Thornton Wilder tells about a traveling salesman who has absurd adventures because he clings to the ethics he knew when he was converted as a 1920 undergraduate. These ethics include never using force to resist evil, even burglars; marrying the first girl you sleep with; accosting strangers on the state of their souls; writing scriptural texts on hotel blotters to the annoyance of room clerks; and never using banks, because they practice usury. Naturally this salesman gets into ridiculous trials but keeps on saying that his religion cost him a lot and he is not going to lose it. "I didn't put myself through college for four years and go through a difficult religious conversion in order to have the same ideas as other people have." He knows God by direct experience, but his thinking does not match his mysticism. His morality is frozen at the point he reached in college; in his Christianity, there is no Holy Spirit. The title page of the book has a quotation from an earlier Wilder novel, *The Woman of Andros*: "Of all forms of genius, goodness has the longest awkward age."

Mysticism by itself is not too much God but too little
duty. It is in a sense like cirrhosis of the liver, which some
doctors say is caused not by too much alcohol but by too
little food, a vitamin deficiency. Or, using the model of the
mind as a black box receiving inputs and giving outputs:
mysticism is an essential input if the system is to function
properly, but other things must also go into the black box—
ideas, ideals, beauty, love—or the output will be what behavioral scientists call garbage.

In sum, becoming aware of God bristles with difficulties,
as did a preacher's sermons years ago in a New Haven
church. He began every one of them in the customary way
by giving out his text, announcing his topic, and invariably
adding, "This subject is bristling with difficulties." He
would then proceed to enumerate them. After some time,
the bell in Yale Chapel would toll, and the undergraduates
in his congregation would realize that the college service
was ending and begin to shuffle their feet. Whereupon the
preacher would stop abruptly with "Time admonisheth me
to bring my discourse to a close," and his congregation
would go out one more Sunday with one more subject bristling with difficulties.

To help my reader escape any such fate with mysticism,
I will bring my chapter to a close by outlining one ancient
and sure way to grow in the knowledge of God. It is to keep
the Sabbath. Not surprisingly, this practice too has a label
that has become a libel:

Sabbatarianism

Once every week, Christians quit all routine to give a
whole day to waiting on the Spirit. It is the Sabbath, originally a Jewish holy day (Saturday), changed by the first
Christians from the seventh day of the week to the first
(Sunday), because on that day Jesus rose from the dead.

Its wild hope matches E. E. Cummings's description of an amazing day:

> i thank You God for most this amazing
> day:for the leaping greenly spirits of trees
> and a blue true dream of sky;and for everything
> which is natural which is infinite which is yes
>
> (i who have died am alive again today,
> and this is the sun's birthday;this is the birth
> day of life and of love and wings:and of the gay
> great happening illimitably earth)
>
> how should tasting touching hearing seeing
> breathing any—lifted from the no
> of all nothing—human merely being
> doubt unimaginable You?
>
> (now the ears of my ears awake and
> now the eyes of my eyes are opened)

In Sabbath observance, neither Jews nor Christians try to escape from the physical world. Instead they exercise, dress up, have the best meal of the week, enjoy family and friends, and worship together in a congregation. This contrasts with non-Bible mystics, who are withdrawn in their practices and often unkempt in the mistaken notion that physical neglect is evidence of spiritual zeal. Another contrast is that the Bible command to rest one day in each week specifically orders work on the other days, whereas the guru in Asia and America would like to meditate all day, every day. Ideally his whole life of transcendental meditation is planned inaction.

The heart of Sabbatarianism is the gathering in church for about an hour, usually in the morning, with singing, praying, Bible reading, preaching, and for many, partaking of the Lord's Supper. It is the rite of Sunday worship known as "Sunday Go to Meetin' " in country places. The Bible commandment is prefaced by "Remember!" because rest may be forgotten in numbing labor, and labor may be forgotten in play or abstraction. "If I have not forgotten what the inside of a church is made of . . . the inside of a church!"

Sabbatarianism got its bad name because in Victorian homes children were brought up to go to church three times on Sunday, to dress in somber clothes, and to refrain from exercise or from reading anything but lives of the saints. And in the public domain there were laws that prohibited work or athletic contests and in general established a pattern of life that was not agreeable to everyone. It was the *exaggeration* of quiet that was objected to; a moderate disengagement from weekday toil is desirable and is the accepted role in civilized societies. People get relief when a vast leisure settles on their community.

The modern Sabbath is often turned into a nervous, unquiet day, made possible by the automobile and telephone. Parents get up later than usual, take the children to religious school, return home to read the papers, pick up the family, drive to Grandma's to lunch, hurry home for touch football or swimming, take in a late afternoon party, have supper, and perhaps at the end sing hymns with devout friends. The day is interrupted by religious activities, but it violates the first principle of true Sabbath observance which is "No fuss."

Keeping the Sabbath is ordered twice in the Bible, each time with a different reason—one humanitarian, the other psychological. The humanitarian reason is that "thou wast a servant in the land of Egypt" (*Deuteronomy* 5:15). Since you know how awful a seven-day work week is, do not make other people work it. The commandment lists in some detail those who shouldn't work on the Sabbath: "Thou, nor thy son, nor thy daughter, nor thy manservant, nor thy maidservant, nor thine ox, nor thine ass, nor any of thy cattle, nor thy stranger that is within thy gates." No one. Important people always have had time to rest, but God intends it for the unimportant also, "that thy manservant and thy maidservant may rest as well as thou." Making leisure possible for everyone is part of the Golden Rule of doing unto others as ye would they should do unto you. A former generation had cold meals on Sunday so the cook of the household would be free, and colleges used to open on Tuesday instead of Monday so railroad men would not have to work on Sunday running the trains. In an industrial civilization, not everyone can have the same day off, and most workers now have two days off. Which days do not matter as long as one day is their Sabbath. Our current laws on weekly working hours are a social victory made possible partly through Sabbatarian promptings.

The psychological reason for observing the Sabbath is that you need rest just as much as your workers do. Keeping the Sabbath provides not only physical rest for underdogs but also mental rest for overdogs, going back to the awesome creation story in which God Himself rested after He made the universe (*Exodus* 20:11). (The Jewish Sabbath is kept on Saturday after the week's work.) Never mind whether the First Cause made the world in one week or why He should ever need to rest. Like a defensive back running around the interference and grabbing the ball carrier by one ankle, I fasten on this: the most impressive way to insist that rest is part of the cosmic structure is to picture the Creator as resting, and rest therefore becomes necessary for all His creatures.

Native bearers on African safaris say the body must stop walking so the soul can catch up with it. The human nervous system is related to the physical universe; it has a built-in biological clock. All life came out of the sea; man still has in his body the rhythm of the tides as they respond to the moon. Its waxing and waning take place every twenty-eight days, and the female menstrual period may be related to it. The earliest device for telling time was by the moon's four distinct quarters, a change every seven days. This changing sign in the sky suggested that human routine should be renewed every seven days. Sunday is recreation in the literal sense of re-creation, repeating the first Creation, "when the morning stars sang together, and all the sons of God shouted for joy" (*Job* 38:7). Here are the words of an ancient Jewish hymn sung at the evening meal at the beginning of the Sabbath:

> Treasure of heart for the broken people,
> Gift of new soul for the souls distrest,
> Soother of sighs for the prisoned spirit—
> The Sabbath of rest.
> This day is for Israel light and rejoicing,
> A Sabbath of rest.

The prohibition of work one day a week is one of the Ten Commandments, found surprisingly on the same level with the prohibition of murder, adultery, stealing, and lying, the four dramatic wrongdoings that cause the public concern over lawlessness. But the supposedly innocuous neglect of Sunday is the breach in the commandments that opens to all the others. Anti-Sabbatarianism may be a hidden cause of the crime wave. The old-fashioned Sabbath at least gave everyone a chance to wonder What It Was All About, a question that occurs to peddlers as well as to professors. Failure to remember to keep holy the Sabbath day results slowly in a deterioration of personality, a phrase as gruesome as what it describes. It is the root of meaninglessness, the horror of being a peppercorn, and may not be unrelated to street crime.

"Blue Domers" is an amusing description of those who claim they worship on Sunday under the blue dome of nature instead of in church, but the habit itself does not have amusing results when persisted in over the years. Long-continued secular weekends are known in medicine as "the syndrome of the holiday dumps" and are a favorite time for suicide. Without God, the open country or the empty city are emotional dead ends; both natural beauty and urban stillness are depressing if the quiet has no ultimate meaning. Wordsworth's "Dear God! the very houses seem asleep" has to be addressed to Someone.

Jesus said, "The Sabbath was made for man" (*Mark* 2:27), and keeping it is obviously beneficial to our neighbors and to ourselves. But people persist in it not because they believe it is healthful but because they believe it to be God's awesome command. All Christians (not only Roman Catholics) are required to go to church, in city and country, winter and summer. And let's admit frankly, there are disappointments in it.

"Why do I go? Here's why," was the title of an article by Walter Kerr, drama critic of the *New York Times*:

It is quite remarkable how successfully we manage to keep in our heads, simultaneously, two entirely different things: the *church* as we imagine it to be, and the *church* as it is. You see, we really know the facts all the time. We know that most *church* is humdrum, if not a good bit worse than that; we can be fairly certain, on setting off for *church*, that the experience will be less than world-shaking. Yet we always go with that world-shaking sense alive and alert, ready to be tapped, begging to be tapped.

Of course, Mr. Kerr never wrote this paragraph. Cross out *church* and write *theater* to learn what he really wrote. The hazards of churchgoing are like the hazards of theatergoing.

Nevertheless, attending church is the initial step toward becoming aware of God. What alternative is there for a despondent friend who has found he cannot live by bread alone? Will you send him to a doctor you once knew? (He may be dead.) Or give him a book that changed your life? (Perhaps it's out of print.) Or tell him about a school you went to? (He is too old.) Or could psychoanalysis help him? (He cannot commit himself to it.) These and other cures go through the mind and might be possible. But the one easily available is to go to church. If he lives where there are several churches, suggest that he shop around; but if there is only one, that has to be it. Warn him not to be put off by the first cold plunge. If worship sounds too formidable, advise him simply to be inside the building for an hour on Sundays when the congregation is there. Above all, encourage him to stop overactivity on weekends. The cry, "For God's sake, don't just stand there—do something!" can be reversed with the same intensity: "For God's sake, don't just do something—stand there!"

Expect the Spirit. The difference He makes in death and life, disappointment and success, sickness and health, sorrow and joy is apt to be found first in public worship. Going to church as the heart of Sunday brings many good things like encouraging others, pleasing the family, training of children, upholding standards, and seeing friends. But far beyond these, God Himself will be found, the Almighty, the Alpha and Omega, the Beginning and Ending, the Saviour, Source of every blessing.

O God, our help in ages past,
   Our hope for years to come,

Our shelter from the stormy blast,
   And our eternal home:

Under the shadow of thy throne
   Thy saints have dwelt secure;
Sufficient is thine arm alone,
   And our defence is sure.

Before the hills in order stood,
   Or earth received her frame,
From everlasting thou art God,
   To endless years the same.

Three

SACRAMENTALISM

Using Sacraments and Seasons

The Sunday worship just described is a fourth rite to be added to the three in Chapter One: marriage, ordination, and healing of body. Now I'll discuss four more: baptism, confirmation, healing of mind, and the Lord's Supper (Holy Communion, Mass, Eucharist—all the same rite). The ninth, burial, comes in the last chapter under Easter. These nine rites are common to all Christian bodies. Seven of these rites are called sacraments by Roman Catholics; they do not count the funeral or Sunday worship (unless it is the Lord's Supper). Only two are considered sacraments by most Protestants: baptism and the Lord's Supper, although the great Protestant reformer Martin Luther wanted to add a third, penance, the old name for healing of mind.

The word *sacrament* is rejected altogether by some Protestants, who prefer to use the term "ordinance of the Lord" for fear that *sacrament* encourages magic. They point out sadly that hocus-pocus is a corruption of *Hoc est corpus meum*, "This is my body," the words of consecration in the Lord's Supper, and that patter is derived from *Pater Noster*, "Our Father," in the Lord's Prayer.

This tendency of sacraments to degenerate into magic is called sacramentalism. It is the corruption of the rite by the magical idea that it is efficacious no matter what the inner attitude of the participants. But even in this pejorative sense, sacramentalism has value if it warns against abuses. A denigrating remark can light up a custom just as a caricature brings out a character by showing a distortion. The victim of the caricature can correct his distortion when he sees some truth in the way he has been drawn. Thoughtful worshipers are aware of the dangers of magic in the sacraments. *The Book of Common Prayer* has this exhortation:

> Dearly beloved in the Lord, ye who mind to come to the Holy Communion of the Body and Blood of our Saviour Christ, must consider how Saint Paul exhorteth all persons diligently to try and examine themselves, before they presume to eat of that Bread, and drink of that Cup. For as the benefit is great, so is the danger great, if we receive the same unworthily.

Because of such dangers the official number of sacraments has been argued about throughout church history, seven being the number finally settled on until the Reformation of the sixteenth century. Whether the right number of sacraments is seven, three, two, or none, all Christians have continued to use the same nine public occasions for worshiping God, and this similarity is one of the hopes for the eventual reunion of Christendom. As discussed in this book, these nine are:

> Blessing Matrimony
> Ordaining Ministers
> Healing the Body
> Worshiping on Sunday
> Baptizing
> Confirming
> Healing the Mind
> Celebrating the Lord's Supper
> Burying the Dead

Baptism

In baptizing, water is always used; the candidate is immersed, or the water is sprinkled or poured on his head while his name is pronounced with an invariable invocation of the Trinity: "I baptize thee in the Name of the Father, and of the Son, and of the Holy Ghost" (or Holy Spirit, which is the same thing). Christening is another term for baptizing, hence the name or names given in the sacrament are called the Christian names as distinct from the surname (family name) the person is born with. Christening a new ship, however, by breaking a bottle of champagne on her bow is not naming in Christ but is a survival of pagan wine-pouring to the gods. "Come and christen our new barbecue grill" is only asking friends to give the thing a happy start by being present the first time it is used.

Baptism is not original with Christianity. It was a Jewish practice symbolizing beginning again by washing. The Jewish faith (and ours) began with their escape from Egyptian slavery through the Red Sea and across the Jordan River. As they began a new life by escaping through water, so each person begins his life in God through water symbolically washing away the slavish past. The pleasure of bathing was perhaps another reason for the evolution of the bath as a religious rite. In the hot Mediterranean world with no indoor plumbing, washing was rare and exhilarating, a physiological reminder of a psychological fact, the good feeling of God. The font, which holds the baptismal water in a church, comes from the same root as fountain, and recalls that the earliest baptisms were held in streams of running water. It is still the custom to pour the water into the font at the last minute after the congregation has gathered, to suggest moving, cleansing water.

Baptism is sometimes administered under unfavorable

circumstances—in churches to wailing infants, in houses with the muffled popping of champagne corks from the pantry, in hospitals with busy nurses waiting, at crowded Sunday worship, where the congregation cannot see or hear what is happening. Adults are sometimes baptized in outdoor streams with passers-by gawking, or aboard Navy ships with the captain holding the book upside down. In spite of occasional awkwardnesses, baptism is universally practiced by Christians and has always been the initiatory rite of the Christian Church. Its ancient truths are still widely appropriated. Four of them can be grouped under contemporary catchwords:

1. *Existentialism.* This is a fashionable term for an old truth that can be grossly caricatured: jump out of a twenty-story window and you will begin to live. The truth behind this much-used tag is that to act is to be alive; to do something is to realize one's own true existence; to decide is to find life's secret. This idea was brought back over a century ago by the Danish lay theologian Sören Kierkegaard, from the Bible's constant call for decision: "How long halt ye between two opinions?" (*1 Kings* 18:21); "He saith unto them, Come and see" (*John* 1:39).

I used to be bothered by the archaic language of one baptismal question: "Dost thou renounce the devil and all his works, the vain pomp and glory of the world, with all covetous desires of the same, and the sinful desires of the flesh, so that thou wilt not follow, nor be led by them?" But as the years go by, and I know myself and my friends better, and the world's slow stain, what other word is there but renounce? Vain pomp, covetous desires, sinful flesh distort *authentic existence* (Kierkegaard's phrase). A human being is an animal, but he is more than an animal because he has a decision-making apparatus in his brain; he can choose as an animal cannot. He realizes his humanity by discriminating, by accepting limits. To be *this* is to be *not that.* Choosing is essential; the person baptized as an infant is later given the chance to choose for himself in the rite of Confirmation.

Again and again through the centuries, many Christians have forbidden infant baptism on the grounds that a baby cannot decide anything. They hold that before a person can be baptized there must be a realized change in the heart, a definite awareness of God. An Episcopal street-corner evangelist used to say that if you get religion without knowing it, you may lose it without missing it. Those who baptize infants acknowledge this danger but point to later Confirmation as the time for the conscious act of decision.

2. *Anonymous*. Meanwhile, by baptism the infant has been taken into the family of God; in his new baptized life he is supported by parents, godparents, relatives, and friends. It is widely known that members of Alcoholics Anonymous uphold each other; it is not so well known that in this mutual support they are copying Christian practice and that A.A. was founded in a parish church, Calvary, New York City. The Church is *people*, not a building. (This kind of distinction is indicated by a subtle sign over the front door of one club: "House of the Harvard Club of Boston.") Inspired by the success of A.A., there is now a G.A. (Gamblers Anonymous), Synanon (Drug Addicts Anonymous), and O.A. (Overeaters Anonymous). They all have the characteristic that the members reinforce each other through the group. "Anonymous" in these associations primarily stands for the fact that people rarely know the names of any others in the group, but the word in addition has acquired an entirely different meaning having nothing to do with anonymity: it proclaims that the members take care of each other. In this secondary sense of the word, the Church is Christians Anonymous. Therefore, to be baptized is to be grafted into a caring company. At a baptism, the congregation often gathers around the font to dramatize the fact that the new Christian's life will be sur-

rounded by helpers. Baptism is not only the washing away
of the slavish past of humanity; it is also admission into a
concerned fellowship.

The psychologist who said, "Baptize only one of my
twins; I want to use the other as a control," was making fun
of magic, not of baptism. (A control is an exact copy
treated differently from the original in order to see whether
they differ from each other because of the treatment.) How
could one twin be a control unless it had a different environment from the baptized twin? Would the father take
only one child to Sunday school? Have bedside prayers
with only one? Keep the unbaptized child away from meals
until grace had been said? Later would he send them to
different colleges, one with a chapel and one without? Or
would he change the experiment and expose both his twins
to the "company, villainous company" that had been the
spoil of Falstaff, to determine whether the baptized one
would be magically protected? Upbringing is an extension
of baptism.

3. *Genes*. Heredity is as important as upbringing in de-
termining character, even though we do not know as much
about it. It is always a puzzle which remote ancestor gives
a child a particular trait. Geneticists will press on trying to
forecast from great-grandparents exactly what the offspring
will be like. If they succeed, horse racing will cease because
speed will exactly equal bloodlines. But until that time,
human parents, like racing fans, will be faced with the age-
old fact that the newborn is a mysterious package not exactly like any ancestor or sibling. The child comes from
God with a certain originality in his disposition and abili-
ties. This givenness is his pattern of genes or his character,
his true name in the Bible sense. The Hebrews changed
people's names when their characters changed, and that is
why names alter in Scripture: Jacob to Israel, Saul to Paul,
Simon to Peter. We cannot know God's name for a child, so
we call him after a relative or friend. But by baptizing him,

we acknowledge that God has a name for him—his individuality, his life, and his career. The child is only lent to his parents, and they guess this even when they do not reason it out. When mothers and fathers bring their baby for baptism, they are unconsciously saying, "God, take our child, he is really Yours."

4. *Zen.* This is a branch of Buddhism known in America because of its novel way of presenting the old truth that we must wait upon Whatever Is, which moves to us and cannot be compelled by our efforts. If it could be compelled, that would be magic; we can only ask and be passive. *Zen in the Art of Archery* is a primer that solemnly asserts that the way to hit the target is not to aim for it. *The New Yorker* magazine applied this counsel to a more familiar sport in an article entitled "Zen in the Art of Lawn Tennis," and said with tongue in cheek that the way to serve aces is to try to serve double faults. The serious point of Zen is that human effort is not enough.

Translated into Christian terms, Reality is not It but He; and He acts when we are helpless. But, as Zen says, we cannot force Him, and as Christians add, we don't need to; God wants us more than we want Him. If psychiatry is right that rejection is a chief cause of mental suffering, baptism removes that unhappiness by making plain that God comes to us; He accepts us without performance and forgives sin as water washes off dirt. In moments of discouragement a Christian says to himself, "I have been baptized." He remembers his own baptism or, if he was an infant, he has a photograph of it (how young his parents looked!), and he "sees across the earthly years this day as victory's sign." The baptized child is in the Kingdom before he chooses it because God has taken him in. He might grow up never knowing the time when he was not a Christian. For God's initiative we can only wait, a truth grasped under a novel name like Zen by many who missed it in parish sermons and college religion classes.

"Original sin" is theological shorthand for the same thing: that man has an inherited tendency to go wrong; that he needs God to start him toward the good; that he cannot take the initiative himself.

When Christian deviationism insists on the opposite, as in Pelagius's heresy or in Jean Jacques Rousseau's Noble Savage theory, and maintains that man is naturally good, the idea seems plausible. But in moments of terrible insight it is seen to be unfounded. Psychologist C. G. Jung called Adam and Eve a racial archetype—that is, a primordial tale that precisely illustrates the human condition: incompleteness without God. Baptism is, therefore, not so much our dedication of the child to God as it is God's coming to the helpless child as Christ came to the world when it was helpless.

> O loving wisdom of our God!
> When all was sin and shame,
> A second Adam to the fight
> And to the rescue came.
>
> —*Cardinal Newman*

Confirmation

The earliest Christians were baptized only as adults, after they had made their decision for Christ. There was no baptism of infants. But as the Church became a persecuted brotherhood and the bonds between its members became almost like family ties, parents sensed that their young children should also be included. And let's face it, there was an element of magic in this compulsion to baptize infants, and this superstition has persisted: in colonial America the missionaries sneaked behind Iroquois squaws and baptized their papooses with saliva from their tongues!

We all owe much to the Baptists for their continuing protest against the dangers of infant baptism. Baptists are descended from the Anabaptists, who insisted, long before the Reformation, on rebaptizing all adults who had been baptized as infants. John Bunyan was a Baptist. So was Henry Dunster, second president (and real founder) of Harvard, who left his beloved college on principle when he began to disapprove of infant baptism, and went into exile with Roger Williams, the Baptist pioneer of Rhode Island.

It is fair to say, however, that over the centuries the majority of Christian parents have brought their infants to baptism without superstition. Any lingering magic is minimized by godparents (sponsors), who make the decisions and take the vows for the baby. Later, when the young Christian reaches the age of responsibility, he affirms these promises if by then, on his own, he wants to follow Christ. That essential second rite is Confirmation, the word used also in plane reservations. I don't say this flippantly; words mean the same in both secular and religious context unless there is a subconscious motive for obscuring them. Are you going or not? Will you confirm? Do you now promise to follow Christ as your Lord and Saviour, the promise your godparents once made for you?

In the first Christian baptisms were two chief actions: the immersion of the person in water and the placing of hands on his head in blessing. By the fourth century these two parts of the service were separated: the water for baptizing infants, the hands for confirming them later as adults. In churches that use sacramental confirmation, the person first makes his promise (the *sacramentum*, or vow of allegiance) to God before the people. Then he kneels, and the bishop's hands (or the minister's) are placed on his head, the old sign of transmitting God's Spirit. Some denominations do not use the word *confirmation* or actually lay on hands but simply ask mature people to stand before the congregation and profess their faith.

Whatever the rite used, Confirmation emphasizes a new start, surrender, commitment of the will, which is the beginning act of full discipleship. It is the decision asked for in both the baptism of infants and the confirmation of those baptized as babies. I keep jumping between the two rites because everything depends on the age at which baptism takes place. We could say that Baptism and Confirmation are really one service in two parts, divided in time for those baptized as infants, and that therefore a person baptized as an adult does not also need to be confirmed, although he often is. If so, he has twice publicly recorded his commitment to Christ. No harm in that!

Some branches of Christendom now go to the opposite extreme and wish to "confirm" infants at the time they are baptized, thus eliminating any mature commitment. In such practice Confirmation loses its literal meaning, "to reaffirm," and the person never confesses Christ before others. If the human will is left out, the sacrament has been reduced to magic, for *decision* is the key to Baptism and Confirmation.

Using the will brings a powerful enhancement of life, as shown by an interview with Irving Berlin in *Time* magazine, after his bout with an inexplicable depression in middle life.

I invited him to lunch one day to talk over the kind of story we might do about his new musical, *Mr. President*. I was astounded. He never looked better—debonair, rested, and happily worried. I wanted above all to ask one question. I didn't know how to. Finally, I got it out, awkwardly. "After so many years of feeling so—so bad, what cured you?"

He laid it on the table, matter-of-factly: "I decided."

"You decided?"

"That's all."

He spelled it out for me a little. "One night before I

went to sleep, I decided that when I woke up in the morning I would start something and finish it. I was tired of pulling out of everything. Tired of letting people down, letting myself down."

Tom Prideaux, the reporter who asked these questions, adds, "I had expected a far more complex explanation, something subtly psychological, or even religious." Actually, he got what he had expected, for decision is complex, psychological, and religious.

More recently, a Harvard commencement speech by a young man from Brooklyn, Joseph Sorrentino, had the title *Calculus and Spirit*, which sounded like one more account of how computers determine character. Instead, the speaker launched into an account of his ludicrous failures in schools and jobs, culminating in a general discharge from the U.S. Marines.

In a bleach factory, at age fourteen, on my first day, trying to impress my employer, I attempted to carry ten gallons of bleach to a truck we were loading. We lost all ten. At sixteen I worked in a sweater factory where I had the embarrassing experience of being awakened from a nap by the president of the company. My next opportunity came through a furniture company's ad which read: "Wanted, ambitious young man who seeks responsibility." After a month of aligning the wheels on tea carts I got tired of responsibility. Then I became associated with a Wall Street firm—in its messenger department. A shoe factory followed. Here I was so low in the company that the office girls wouldn't let me address them by their first names.

Suddenly the speaker's life changed. He went to night school, re-enlisted in the Marines, got a college degree, *magna cum laude*, and on this particular day was graduating from Harvard Law School. "Do not look for love, tragedy, or trauma to explain this change," he said. "It was simply a resolution from within."

Stewart Alsop, the columnist, several months before the end of his struggle with cancer, had an operation, the results of which discouraged his doctors. Four nights later, semiconscious, he found himself in the corridor of his hospital room dreaming he was on the Baltimore train platform. As he describes it in *Newsweek*:

> I said in a firm authoritative voice, "We won't stop here; start up the train and carry on." The next day the able young doctor in charge of my case told me that he might be imagining things, but the X-rays of my lungs looked a bit better—certainly no worse. The day after, he said there was no doubt about it—the infiltrate was receding. Why? The doctors say frankly they don't know, though they all have a favorite guess. I have a favorite guess, too. My guess is that my decision not to stop at Baltimore had something to do with it. In a kind of fuzzy, hallucinated way, I knew when I announced the decision that it was a decision not to die.

In spite of such instances, the importance of the human will is sometimes overlooked in the Church. Criticism of evangelism is in the grand tradition; the consensus (as Felicia Lamport wrote in *Scrap Irony*) unfortunately too often is:

> The refined
> mind
> Will conceal
> zeal.

But every time the Church renews itself, it always returns to what Kierkegaard called the "Leap of Faith."
Leaders as diverse as Protestant revivalists and Passionist
Fathers ask people to choose. A mission or retreat aims for
the will, as do groups like the Salvation Army, the Inter-
Varsity Christian Fellowship, Moral Rearmament, and the
Pentecostals. Many churches have revivals every year for
recommitment of their regular members. It is what the old
lady had in mind when she was being conducted through
the Washington Cathedral: "I don't care who is buried
here, what I want to know is, has anyone been converted in
this building lately?" Her reticent Episcopal Church asks
an intensely personal question at both baptism and confirmation: "Do you promise to follow Jesus Christ as your
Lord and Saviour?" Its invitation to the Lord's Supper is
equally intimate: "Ye who do truly and earnestly repent . . .
and intend to lead a new life . . . draw near with faith."

A decision made once in a lifetime at a public service of
baptism or confirmation may be repeated in private over
and over. If once-born souls are those who never knew the
time when they were not Christian, the twice-born need not
be born only twice but can be reborn many times. The
short acts of the will can never be contrasted with the long
years of steady growth; psychologically they merge. Quick
decisions can lead to lifelong patterns. "Ships that pass in the
night" is not a melancholy metaphor among believers.
Chance contacts lighten the darkness; people we meet only
once communicate courage to us and we to them. A fleeting
encounter can alter life, as John Bunyan suggests by the
one smile in *Pilgrim's Progress* from "a man that appeared
to me to be a very great and honorable person; his name, as
I remember is Evangelist. . . . He gave me one smile, and
bid me God-speed."

Holy Days and Holidays

Seasons as well as sacraments are means by which the believer increases his awareness of God. The nine rites of the Church are reinforced by special services held annually on holy days. These recall historic events or particular teachings. Christianity has always kept such a calendar of important occasions, many of them inherited directly from Judaism. And like the sacraments, the seasons can fall victim to sacramentalism in its degraded sense—that is, they can be observed as if efficacious in themselves, no matter what the ethics of the observer. A girl on a bus was overheard complaining to her companion how bad she felt from being drunk the night before. She said her mouth tasted like the inside of the bus driver's glove. But when her companion offered her a soothing lozenge, she refused indignantly, "You know I've given up candy for Lent."

Holy days kept thoughtlessly have a tendency to lapse into holidays. Starting in the fall, Halloween on October 31 is the first instance. It is an abbreviation of All Hallows' Eve, the night before All Saints' Day (November 1) and two nights before All Souls' Day (November 2). One day for the saints and one for the rest of us souls were placed in the autumn to distinguish the Christian view of death from the pagan one. Autumn is the season of the dying year: leaves fall, cattle are butchered for the winter, and the increasing cold is hard on older people. So autumn made primitive man think of his dead. At that season he held feasts for them that embodied three pagan beliefs: the dead cannot be recognized; they are ill-disposed to the living; yet they depend on them for food. Today these three melancholy beliefs persist in Halloween pranks. The "ghosts" who ring the doorbell wear masks and costumes to prevent recognition, their threatened tricks signify ill will, and treats of candy show their dependence on the living householder.

Christianity holds exactly opposite opinions about the dead: it believes that they will be recognized in the hereafter, that they mean only good to the living, and that their welfare does not depend on them. To drive home these disagreements, the Church put its double remembrance, All Saints and All Souls, right in the middle of the heathen memorial. And gradually the Christian reminder of heroes and friends made the older picture of the dead seem ridiculous. If there is a future life, there must be continuance of character and disposition, and death would not change a friend into a ghost threatening harm unless bought off with a bribe. In time, this logic displaced the pagan beliefs that survive now in Halloween customs carried on by children unaware of their origin. Yet sometimes the happy picture of the dead brought out by saints and souls is lost by not observing the holy days, while the dreary pagan theories survive on All Hallows' Eve. No churchgoing on the holy days, only ragamuffins on the holiday.

Thanksgiving is another example; it is proclaimed by the President annually as a "Day of Thanksgiving and Prayer" but is abbreviated to "Thanksgiving Day" because public worship is widely ignored. The holy day has become a four-day holiday taken up with football and family reunions. By eliminating prayer, people forget the original purpose of the thanksgiving, which was to thank God for freedom, plenty, and survival in a new land. Ritualism is one good way to remember what ought not to be forgotten. "When ye be come to the land which the Lord will give you . . . ye shall keep this service. And . . . when your children shall say unto you, What mean ye by this service? . . . ye shall say, It is the sacrifice of the Lord's passover, who passed over the houses of the children of Israel in Egypt, when he smote the Egyptians, and delivered our houses" (*Exodus* 12:25–27). In the Western tradition the Passover is the earliest celebration of freedom, as Thanksgiving is the latest. Through worship at Passover the Jews have kept freedom alive for thirty-three centuries, in ghetto and exile. Their spiritual descendants, the Christians, who may not have been to church Thanksgiving morning, reflect uneasily on this as they wait for their grandchildren to arrive and hear the spot news of fresh tyrannies interrupting the televised football game.

Right after Thanksgiving, noisy preparations for Christmas start alongside a quiet preparation called Advent. Stores and streets are decorated; magazines grow bulky with advertisements; cards come with illegible signatures; nostalgic music is heard over loudspeakers; office parties serve warm gin in paper cups; glee clubs sing carols in Latin and Polish; and service clubs have Christmas programs. Generally, work is heavier and the children's social life occupies conscientious parents. Both Christian and pagan complain happily about the Christmas rush, with a common refrain, "As soon as the holidays are over." All this celebrating is not due to Christmas; parties and gifts were common in midwinter long before Jesus's birth. Christmas is one holy day that began as a holiday and still is only a holiday for many. It lasts twelve days, as we sing:

The twelfth day of Christmas my true love gave to me
  . . . and a partridge in a pear tree.

The Epiphany season, which follows, lasts four to seven weeks. By this large time difference between twelve days and many weeks, the church calendar emphasizes that when Christ is born (Christmas), he must immediately be shown forth (Epiphany). After Epiphany come two months of Pre-Lent and Lent, ending with Easter. The three Sundays of Pre-Lent are Septuagesima, Sexagesima, and Quinquagesima, Latin derivatives for roughly seventy, sixty, and fifty days before Easter. These ancient names may be given up in the new church calendars. This would be a pity, because they bring out the point that everything dates from Easter and that Pre-Lent and Lent are part of Easter. Austerity is part of happiness. "The rule of duty and the rule of joy seem to me all one," said Oliver Wendell Holmes. Church seasons and the colors on the altar told people long before they could read or write that Pre-Lent begins the celebration of the Resurrection.

Occasionally the secularist has the feeling that Lenten self-denial is more symbolic than actual, when he is confronted with lobster Newburgh, shad roe, and soft-shelled crabs at the meatless tables of some of his punctilious friends. Along with his doubts about abstinence, however, he remembers tales of his great-grandparents who came to America in immigrant ships or went West in covered wagons. They used to say they could never have stood the hardships except by being narrow-minded about amusements; theirs was the immense difficulty of preserving culture in the wilderness. In 1636, when it was founded, "Harvard must have been puritan, or could not have existed," wrote Samuel Eliot Morison. "A neo-Platonist could not be a man of action, a pioneer, an emigrant, any more than a Hindu." So the nonchurchman has mixed feelings about Lent; he smiles at it, yet he respects it. It does not surprise him that all churches are not agreed about its value.

The end of Lent is Easter Day, whose eggs and lilies suggest bursting springtime. Easter was the name of a spring goddess, and rabbits, flowers, and baby chicks are leftovers of fertility rites, as the comparative study of religions teaches quite correctly. But Easter comes in the spring only in the northern hemisphere; in the southern hemisphere it comes in the autumn. There is no necessary connection between springtime and Christ's rising from the dead. An Easter sermon that ignored the point of the day was pilloried by George Santayana in his novel *The Last Puritan*:

The sermon on the Resurrection might prudently avoid all mention of Christ or the Trump of Doom startling the Dead out of the grave. Instead the preacher might blandly describe the resurrection of nature in the spring, the resurrection of science in the modern world, and the resurrection of heroic freedom in the American character.

As he listened, the Last Puritan

> ... shrewdly added for his own benefit that spring was a dangerous season for catching colds; that ideas revived from time to time in the world were chiefly fallacies, since sound notions never died out; and that the best people in America were not heroes, but thrifty, respectable citizens of the old British stock.

Santayana's imaginary sermon is matched every year by real-life sermons that are equally irrelevant.

One widespread Easter custom is the wearing of new clothes, possibly because they give courage, as new hats were said to cheer women (before they stopped wearing them). Or possibly because some Edwardians wore every new article of clothing first to church on Sunday and this was expanded into the notion that on Easter Day all clothing must be new. A better explanation is that in the primitive Church, new converts were baptized on Easter Day and had new white togas for the occasion. Another minor folkway is hiding colored eggs for the children to find, one of the links with the Jewish Passover, when old leaven is hidden around the house for children to discover and throw away so only new leaven will greet the holy day. Such customs are not widespread; families are busy with church-going, so there are few secondary traditions except for decorating their churches with flowers. Easter Day (never called by its pagan name, Sun-day) has few customs because the resurrection of Christ is unrelated to anything that ever happened before. Believers are trying each year to grasp the uniqueness of what took place on the Third Day.

Pentecost, fifty days after Easter, is not as widely observed as Christmas and Easter even though, as already mentioned, it constitutes with them the three great holy days of the Christian calendar. What everyone recalls about it was presented once in a tableau of the Bible story (*Acts* 2:1–11) at a pentecostal tabernacle in Los Angeles. The company gathered on the stage were dressed as the first Christians were when the Holy Spirit descended on them. To represent the cloven tongues of fire in which the Spirit came, kerosene-soaked wads of cotton were lighted and let down with wires on the unfortunate actors. The lively effect produced by the dripping kerosene recaptured the original occasion when the spirit-filled Christians shouted in tongues and were thought to be drunk. Pentecostal hysteria today often arouses a like misgiving. Was it British distrust of it that made them call Pentecost by the neutral name, Whitsunday (White Sunday, because those baptized that day wore white)? Today in England Whitmonday and Whittuesday are days off and the holy day has become the Whitsun holiday.

Pentecost begins the longest season of the Christian calendar, continuing through the summer and autumn until December, when Advent starts a New Year. Pentecost season is called Trinity by many Christians. Both names are good because the Pentecostal spirit and hard thinking about faith are equally essential.

Holy days merge into holidays when their initial impulse fades, and the psychological consequences of the fading are serious. The mind (Hippocrates again) has sacred times as well as sacred places. In *The Eighth Day*, Thornton Wilder's novel about survival, a Catholic bishop tells of being imprisoned in Asia with other missionaries for so long that they forgot what time of year it was. Then a new prisoner arrived who told them the date, "and we got back our days, our Sundays and our Easter and our Feast Days—that other calendar that strengthens our steps and confirms our joys." A man and wife so poor they were sleeping in an automobile parked on New York streets reported that they were demoralized because they had lost track of the calendar. It is a nuisance to misplace an engagement book for a few days, but it is shattering to anyone's psyche to lose Christmas, Easter, and the children's birthdays. The human race depends on times of remembrance and renewal; culture comes from cult. Families are knit together by anniversaries. I tell brides and grooms I marry to memorize Yeats's *Prayer for My Daughter*:

> And may her bridegroom bring her to a house
> Where all's accustomed, ceremonious;
> For arrogance and hatred are the wares
> Peddled in the thoroughfares.
> How but in custom and in ceremony
> Are innocence and beauty born?

When sculptress Malvina Hoffman made a series of heads to illustrate ethnic characteristics, she was eager to get the Ubangi women in the side show of a circus to pose. Her secretary traced them to a small hotel, where she found them (with their many brass rings around their long necks) playing bridge and smoking black cigars. Through an interpreter she asked them to pose the following Sunday morning, their day off. They refused. She doubled and then redoubled the fee, but still the puzzling answer was they couldn't. Finally, the interpreter told her the literal translation of their refusal which completely baffled him: "They seem to be saying they have a date with the Virgin Mary." It dawned on the secretary that they were Roman Catholics who, despite their primitive theology, at least knew they had a firm appointment every Sunday "where all's accustomed, ceremonious." A Protestant Chief of Naval Operations used to say, "I think I'll go to church Sunday if the weather holds." This was a family joke because the weather made no difference to a blue-water sailor.

Healing of the Mind

Returning to ritualisms, the seventh in our list is the curing of mental distress. The Church has a specific for psychic ailments, in the sense that medicine speaks of a specific for a physical ailment—that is, a particular cure for a particular disease: for heart trouble, digitalis; for malaria, quinine; for infection, penicillin. In addition, doctors urge one overall cure, which is rest (except in the Navy, where the prescription for everything is castor oil). The specific for mental distress is repentance. Solzhenitsyn said it is the only starting point for spiritual growth. This is the ancient sacrament of penance, the rite Martin Luther wanted to include as the third sacrament for Protestants, in addition to baptism and the Lord's Supper. Its locus is the confessional box, the pastor's study, and the general confession made by the whole congregation: "We have left undone those things which we ought to have done; And we have done those things which we ought not to have done; And there is no health in us."

Repentance is Christianity's overall cure for what Santayana called "unspirit and infinite annoyance," and before that it was Judaism's. The Jew first discovered this connection between peace of mind and reform of character. "The morbid Jewish preoccupation with sin" was one of Hitler's reasons for hating the Jews. As a matter of fact, this preoccupation is not Jewish but universal, and it is not morbid, because the accent is not on sin but on forgiveness. "Come now, and let us reason together, saith the Lord: though

"*Now, there goes a happy man, the damn fool.*"

Drawing by Stan Hunt; © *1972, The New Yorker Magazine, Inc.*

your sins be as scarlet, they shall be as white as snow"
(*Isaiah* 1:18).

"Why are there so many Jews in psychoanalytic medicine?" is a question Sigmund Freud once asked, and it has
been raised in medical journals. It is used as an ethnic putdown, yet the answer to the question is one of Israel's glories: the Jew is a child of a Book that sees existence as a
fight against all evil because evil denies people the joy of
God. The Ten Commandments are age-old experience in

conduct; psychiatry is a fresh approach to the same subject. Both are concerned with moving men toward what religion calls holiness and psychiatry calls wholeness, words having the same root, the Anglo-Saxon *hāl* (healthy, sound, well). Whether the remaking of human nature is toward holiness or wholeness, Jews have devoted themselves to it through their faith and ethics for four thousand years. Jewish psychoanalysts, even when they are irreligious, inherit a racial bent toward religion and morality. "It's absolutely essential that we look not at what psychiatrists say they do; but at what they actually do," writes a distinguished practitioner. "They are not concerned with mental illnesses and their treatments. In practice, they deal with personal, social, and ethical problems in living."

The chief personal, social, and ethical problems in living are meaninglessness and addiction; again Shakespeare's peppercorn and brewer's horse. The peppercorn, the dried berry of the pepper plant, is so small it becomes a symbol of futility. In reality, it is not useless, but if a man thinks his life is useless, that comes to the same thing. In Shakespeare's day the brewer's horse was not the magnificent Clydesdale pulling an enormous truck of beer barrels in teams of eight (whence comes the temperance song, "The brewer's big horses can't run over me"). What Falstaff knew was the single emaciated beast with belly swollen from having been fed the unsold beer. The pathetic sixteenth-century brewer's horse represents any obsession that distorts existence (alcohol, drugs, gambling, overeating, lust). To paint with a broad brush, all psychic ailments are caused by meaninglessness or addiction.

Again painting with a broad brush, the cure is repentance, and the initial step toward this is not to forget what the inside of a church is made of. Shakespeare was not referring to the materials of construction, oak or pine, brass or silver ornaments, but to the Church's inner workings. Where in these inner workings does repentance come alive?

A place rarely used any longer was the open meeting where wrongdoing was acknowledged to the whole congregation. "Confess your faults one to another, and pray one for another, that ye may be healed" (*James* 5:16). (As in the contemporary AA meeting.) "Many of them that believed came, and confessed, and showed their deeds" (*Acts* 19:18).

There is both power and danger in public confession, and throughout the ages it is always being stopped and revived. After many centuries, auricular confession (in the ears of a priest alone) became more customary. This is not confession to a priest but confession to God in the presence of a priest. Auricular confession was made compulsory by the Church during the twelfth century and has continued to be compulsory for Roman Catholics; after the Reformation it was made voluntary for Protestants. The Protestant decision about this kind of confession was: none must, all may, some should, a permissiveness defended by Louis Bouyer, a Roman Catholic theologian who had been a Protestant:

> To many Roman Catholics, the assertion of Protestants that they do not confess to man but to God is only a euphemistic way of saying that they do not confess at all. To Protestants, on the other hand, confession to God is a constant awareness that God sees us and tests us, which is the most severe and inescapable of all the obligations that religion or ethics could impose. The serious Protestant conscience that has never confessed through a man is often a noble thing.

As sacramental confession is practiced, it is usually made in a small private booth inside the church. Even if it is denigrated as ritualism, it has value because it is routine and without embarrassment. The priest hears the sins the penitent recites, gives God's absolution if he believes him repentant, prescribes restitution if possible, and orders a penance freely accepted by the sinner. Repentance and penance sound alike and are often confused, but they are not the same. Repentance is contrition for sin, being honest with oneself, asking God to create a new person. Penance is a punishment willingly undertaken to help the sinner atone for his sin and thus to deepen his repentance.

The danger of auricular confession is that it tends to leave moral decisions to the priest, who does not know all the pertinent facts. Only the penitent living a particular life is aware of its innermost compromises as no one else is. A study called casuistry analyzes special cases by applying ethical principles and deciding how far circumstances alter them; yet no clergyman can understand thoroughly the rights and wrongs of coal mining, child rearing, or repairing television sets. As the washerwoman remarked after a young celibate's sermon on marriage: "I wish to God I knew as little about it as he does."

The core of the danger is that the priest may give absolution too readily, which used to be known as "short shrift" when forgiving was called shriving. The penitent, without meaning to deceive, has not told all the facts to the priest, who does not know enough to probe for marginal wrongdoing. Therefore, to "none must, all may, some should," might be added, "Some should not confess before anyone but should sweat it out for themselves with God alone." Confession through a minister has always been practiced in Protestant churches by what sociologists grandly label "the nonstructured intimacy of preacher and people." Whether to a priest or minister or rabbi, talking to a clergyman is good therapy because it "cleanses the stuffed bosom" and makes more vivid the truth of forgiveness.

Roman Catholics are now being encouraged to consider face-to-face confession and congregational penitential prayers followed by a general absolution. At the same time non-Roman churches are increasingly using auricular confession (or what they call sacramental confession) in the presence of a priest or minister alone.

If this discussion of repentance-penance is complex, it is because peace of mind is complex. If it appears to vacillate between Catholic and Protestant practice, it is because both have value. Justice Felix Frankfurter observed that the law is as untidy as the life with which it deals. This could also be said of theology.

There is even more untidiness: mind and body cannot be separated, because man is both; but healing of mind must be considered separately from healing of body. Christian practice now and always has divided the two cures. Historically, the body's healing was unction, the mind's was penance, two entirely different sacramental actions. To emphasize the distinction, I have separated them in this book. Some readers of the opening chapter, where healing of the body was outlined, may have said to themselves, "Get the brain straightened out and the arthritis will go away." This is only sometimes true. There are sick brains in healthy bodies and healthy brains in sick bodies. The essential point is that God heals body cells as well as brain cells, and sometimes the cures, as far as we can see, are mysteriously unrelated.

The Church stands in a cross fire between spiritualists who claim the brain is all and materialists who claim the body is all. Christian Science exaggerates the brain by maintaining that the body exists only as a projection of the mind. From this standpoint it insists that nothing at all need be done physically for the body; if the mind can be put into order, the body will get well. I repeat that this is sometimes true, but it is a dangerous exaggeration to neglect the body in order to demonstrate the dominance of mind. And I say this sadly, for Christian Science did much to bring healing back into the mainstream of Christian practice. All believers owe a debt to Mary Baker Eddy.

Certain schools of behavioral science go the other way and exaggerate the physical by holding that the mind exists only as a projection of the body, like the phosphorescence on sea waves at sunset. They say that if everyone's glands could be rearranged and given the right injections, the brain would think nothing but beautiful thoughts. This opposite theory is also only sometimes true. But leaving aside the chemistry, the human will is a part of the brain, and the brain can decide to open itself to the influence of a Holy Spirit outside it.

It is interesting that both these extreme positions borrow the word science for their exaggeration—Christian Science and behavioral science—just as the Communists borrow the word science for their socialism, and name it scientific socialism. Scientists observing these misusings of the name *science* are less critical of the frequent misusings of the word *religion*.

A UN soldier in Africa, meeting a tribal medicine man in paint, feathers, and mask, said to his buddy, "He sort of corresponds to our chaplain." He was right, because the primitive medicine man was both minister and doctor. His work has been divided into two healing functions in civilized life, healing of body and healing of mind. Some scholars think these may be only temporary specializations, because they belong together. When physician and minister separated long ago, one took the body and the other the mind, yet each one ever since has kept reaching into the other's area like the poaching of a good doubles team in tennis. To this day, doctors and clergy work together. A man who gets pills from his physician may also get some fatherly talk; and many a man may be told by his minister to sleep and exercise regularly. The Gospel foreshadows this common concern: "Jesus realized instantly what they were thinking, and said to them: 'Why must you argue like this in your minds? Which do you suppose is easier—to say to a paralyzed man, Your sins are forgiven, or Get up, pick up your bed and walk?'" (*Mark* 2:8–9).

It is widely held that psychiatrists do for nonbelievers

what the clergy do for believers, that the couch is the equivalent of the confessional box or the pastor's study. This is too easy a generalization. Doctors and clergy overlap because they care for the same person, and they have overlapped ever since the primitive medicine man was both physician and priest. Doctors care for the sick and incipient sick; the clergy for the incipient sick and the well. Whether the middle group, the incipient sick, should see a doctor or a clergyman requires the combined judgment of doctor, clergyman, and family. The family can never abandon its duty over the long pull, because in general doctors and clergy are for emergencies (partly because there aren't enough of them). The clergy should keep away from the mentally ill unless they have the doctor's express permission. And the psychiatrists should stay away from the substantially well; it is not helpful to prowl in the marshlands of personality. Ministers and doctors are so much a team that the occasional alarm about clergy in the hands of psychiatrists could be matched by alarm over psychiatrists in the hands of the clergy, attending church and listening to their sermons week after week. The two get along together better than the public realizes, because they go back to a common ancestor who used both herbs and tom-tom.

For amateur psychologists (a title I do not use derisively), the way to help anyone suffering from boredom or addiction is to bring up the subject of sin, probably without using this unfashionable word. Yet it is a good short word and there is no precise synonym. It means alienation from God, refusal to be found by Him, hardness of heart. Ask the unhappy person (if he seeks your help) what he thinks he is doing wrong; tell him to go over his compromises privately to himself and to God. He can use his fingers; the number of the commandments may be ten because men ticked them off on their fingers long before the human race could read or write. Perhaps the depressed person should also tell his sins to his clergyman (or to you if he so desires), because talking to someone may show the person that some things he thought were wrong are not wrong at all. He may be the victim of exaggerated conscientiousness (in technical theology, scrupulosity). But where he really is wrong (we are all sinners), confession of it externalizes sin and makes God's forgiveness more understandable. For your part, be willing to listen; perhaps this is your greatest usefulness. The bewildered person need not confess through you or through anyone else, but he must admit his sins to himself and, above all, to God. If he is uncertain about God, like the psychoanalyst I mentioned at the beginning of this book, he will know Him the minute he turns to Him for help.

Because of these golden conversations, friends are important for healing of mind. A leading psychoanalyst once said he never told a patient anything the patient could not have learned from a wise grandmother, and a clergyman might say the same thing. Other sources of help for a peppercorn or brewer's horse are books, drama, sermons, advice-to-the-lovelorn columns, and their own common sense (better after a meal). The Church urges people to take all the nonchurchly avenues by which tranquillity is restored to human life. The priest hearing confession or the minister talking privately is often giving only the last push to a long process by which God has led the penitent through friends, doctors, and his grandmother. Finally, each person stands alone before God, Who made him and loves him.

Every man's birthright is to know that God forgives when man repents. The past is finished; Rudyard Kipling was wrong when he wrote:

> If we fall in the race, though we win
>   The hoof-slide is scarred on the course.
> Though Allah and Earth pardon Sin,
>   Remaineth for ever Remorse.

When Allah pardons, no remorse remains. In today's psychological idiom, the sinner's view of God's forgiveness should be: "I am accepted even though I am unacceptable." God's forgiveness is one of the major experiences of life, the heart of the Good News (Gospel). Forgiveness is a moment of truth more piercing than those tiresomely offered: orgasm, drugs, "copping out," death in the afternoon (or any other time).

> There is a Balm in Gilead
> To make the wounded whole,
> There is a Balm in Gilead
> To heal the sin-sick soul.

The Lord's Supper

Whenever healing of body or peace of mind is mentioned, it is necessary to add crudely that God is not a bottle of pills. He "healeth all thy diseases" and "forgiveth all thine iniquities" (*Psalm* 103:3), but He Himself is a greater boon than either healing. God is also far more to be desired than any prosperity that may come from faith. This sounds pious, and it is said you can't talk pious to the tough any more than you can talk tough to the pious. However it sounds, both healing and prosperity are only by-products of a greater good: the sense of the presence of God.

And let me stress that the by-products do not always come to His followers; which brings the question: if God wants His children to have the good things of life, why doesn't He make them happen? The answer requires deeper thinking than this book provides, but here is a start: God has given man freedom, and part of that freedom has to be the possibility of getting hurt. He is like a mother giving a child a bicycle and thereby exposing him to the chance of an accident. She accepts this chance and limits her control over him because she hopes the bicycle will help him mature. The alternative is the horror story that comes to light when the health authorities find a grown man shut up in one room all his life by a neurotic mother who never let him go out. God's purpose has let men out into a dangerous world. William James described the tie between freedom and danger:

> Suppose that the world's author put the case to you before creation, saying: "I am going to make a world not certain to be saved, a world the perfection of which shall be conditional merely, the condition being that each several agent does its own level best. I offer you the chance of taking part in such a world. Its safety, you see, is unwarranted. It is a real adventure, with real danger, yet it may win through. It is a social scheme of cooperative work genuinely to be done. Will you join the procession? Will you trust yourself and trust others enough to face the risk?" . . . There is a healthy-minded buoyancy in most of us which such a universe would exactly fit. We would therefore accept the offer—*Done! and Done Again!* (From Goethe's *Faust:* If I be quieted with a bed of ease, then let that moment be the end of me. . . . And that's a wager! *Top! und schlag auf schlag!*) It would be just like the world we practically live in; the world proposed would seem "rational" to us in the most living way.

Perhaps the evil we experience cannot be made rational by this or any other line of reasoning, especially to anyone in deep suffering. But the first thing to be said about evil is that God is against it. He wants health of body and mind for all men. "I am come that they might have life, and that they might have it more abundantly" (*John* 10:10) is not metaphysical doubletalk. Jesus does not substitute abstractions for the tangible goods of life but tells their order. "Seek ye first the kingdom of God, and his righteousness; and all these things shall be added unto you" (*Matthew* 6:33). To say that man does not live by bread alone does not mean that bread is unnecessary.

The second thing to be said about evil is that we cannot use God solely as a means to get rid of it. Utilitarianism does not last long in religion, even though people may start by using God only as a tool for help. But when they begin to know Him even a little, that knowledge outweighs any other benefits. And if benefits rarely come, and finally in old age when they disappear altogether, God suffices. Teilhard de Chardin, the Jesuit paleontologist, in *The Divine Milieu* says to Him: "In the life which wells up in me and in the matter which sustains me, I find much more than Your gifts. It is You Yourself whom I find, You who make me participate in Your being, You who mould me."

"I AM" was one of God's ancient Hebrew names (*Exodus* 3:14). Man's response to *Whoever Is* may vary from unconditional obedience to unsteady church attendance on Sunday; but at either extreme the magnet finally is God, not His rewards. "Thou hast put gladness in my heart; yea, more than when their corn and wine and oil increase" (*Psalm* 4:8). The miracle of Lourdes is not those who are healed, but the indescribable happiness on the faces of many who are not healed.

Well, if we say crudely that God is not a bottle of pills, what is He, equally crudely? To repeat, He is not what but Who, and He is Someone Who feeds us. This is the awesome, elementary fact about the Lord's Supper, the central rite of Christian nurture. The two great sacraments of the Christian Church are the homely actions of washing and eating. Sometimes their simplicity is lost in the ceremonial that has grown up around them. One way to begin to understand the Lord's Supper is to relate it to simple things like family dinners, birthday parties, and even, "Let's have lunch together sometime." It is true we often eat with people to persuade them about something or because we will inherit Uncle John's silver, but above all secondary motives is the primary one of happiness in each other's company.

On the night in which he was betrayed, Jesus was at a Passover supper with his intimate friends. He took the unleavened bread, blessed and broke it, and gave it to them, saying, "This is my body, which is given for you." Then he took the cup of wine, and when he had given thanks he said, "Drink ye all of this; for this is my blood which is shed for you." And he added, "Do this in remembrance of me." Ever since, Christians have done this, some every day, more once a week, many once a month, some every quarter, all on the yearly observances of Pentecost, Christmas, and Easter. The frequency of receiving the sacrament is not related to devoutness; how many go how often would be a meaningless statistic. The overriding fact is that the Christian Church has partaken of the Bread and Cup continuously since that night in Jerusalem. So universal is attendance at the Lord's Supper that it is commonly called "The Sacrament" although baptism is of equal importance.

Each of the names for the Lord's Supper emphasizes an aspect of its richness: *Eucharist* is Greek for thanksgiving; *Memorial* brings out the historic in the Last Supper; *Communion* promises fellowship with God, with each other, and all the company of heaven; *Holy Sacrifice* is Christ's death on the cross; *Breaking of Bread* was one of its earliest names (*Acts* 2:42 and 46); the *Agape* (love) suggests the bond of all races and classes. *Holy Mystery* is a confusing name, because mystery in English is a hidden secret whereas the original Greek *mysterion* is a revealed secret. Hence Holy Mystery is not the mysteriousness of the English but the openness of the Greek. It is the last page of a detective story, which clears everything up.

One of the commonest names—*Mass*—arose in a curious way. In medieval days, at the end of the service, the priest said, *Ite, missa est,* the Latin for "Go forth, it is the dismissal," and what was heard by the people was missa . . . miss . . . mass. This name has come to have value just because it is noncommittal; other names emphasize particular aspects and may tend to limit.

But the Lord's Supper is never merely a thanksgiving or memorial or communion, or sacrifice, or revealed mystery. *Merely* is a crippling word in religion; the sacrament that to one person is merely this or merely that may stand for infinite riches to other people at the same service. Hence the advantage of a colorless name like *Mass,* which does not limit. The word used for the Lord's Supper should include every insight and power given by breaking the bread and blessing the cup.

Details of practice vary in Christian churches. In some the communicants come forward to kneel around the altar; in others, they remain in the pews and the sacred elements are brought to them. The wine may be in a common cup called a chalice, or in individual cups. Some churches substitute unfermented grape juice for wine. Ordinary bread may be used; but small wafers of unleavened bread are more customary, to recall the hardship of the Passover escape from Egypt. "Christ our Passover is sacrificed for us: Therefore let us keep the feast, not with old leaven, neither with the leaven of malice and wickedness; but with the unleavened bread of sincerity and truth" (*1 Corinthians* 5:7–8). The Passover bread became the Lord's Supper when Christ spoke the words and distributed the broken bread and the cup he had blessed. To fulfill his command, that much history is always repeated, whatever else is added in solemnity, music, and architecture.

In the early centuries, when people ate only one meal a day, the Lord's Supper was a full meal, not just bread and wine. The physical elation that followed it was greater than is felt now from a wafer and a sip of wine. Like the bath of baptism, the meal of communion gave a sharp physiological reminder of spiritual well-being. In those days bread and wine were staples that were always on the table, and by using them Jesus showed that he intended the Lord's Supper to be habitual, and as independent of our moods as our daily meals. He took just what was ordinarily there, bread and wine; gorgeous vestments and jeweled chalices can never conceal this fact. Holy communion is holy commonness.

The thoughtful observer sometimes thinks Christians attend their rites in a superstitious way, believing that there is magic in the ceremonial even when the mind is disengaged. This attitude would be sacramentalism in its debased form. But a subtle point has been missed. The Christian observes his ritualism and holy days because they ring bells. There is a ministry of memory. William Temple points this out in a paragraph about attendance at Communion when enthusiasm (God within) is gone:

Many of those who set special store by the sacramental mode of worship value it because the efficacy is totally independent of any conscious apprehension or spiritual experience at that time. When faith exists as a struggle to believe in spite of empirical and temperamental pressure to unbelief, when the life of feeling is dead, when nothing is left but stark loyalty to God as He is dimly and waveringly apprehended to be—then the sheer objectivity, even the express materialism, of a sacrament gives it a value that nothing else can have. And when faith revives its ardor, and feeling is once more aglow, when the activity of prayers spoken and praises sung is again a natural expression of devotion, the rite which is believed to have retained its efficacy when all else failed becomes a focus of grateful adoration to the God Who therein offered grace—that is, His love in action—to a soul that could receive Him in no other way.

The custom in the early Church was for everyone to bring what food he could and for everyone to eat what he wanted no matter whether he had brought anything or not. "From each according to his ability, to each according to his need" was the rule at the Lord's Supper long before it became a Communist slogan. From the beginning the poorest could eat without contributing anything. To this day, the bread and wine are sometimes kept on a side shelf, known as the credence table, and are moved to the altar at the time of collecting the offering of the people to symbolize that the food, like the money, is the gift of the congregation. In modern liturgical practice, the bread and wine are often carried in procession with the collection from the back of the church to the altar to make the point more vivid that the congregation has paid for this meal and all are welcome, pay or no pay. Likewise, following ancient practice (in Anglican churches, for instance), the collection taken at the Lord's Supper is often kept for the poor; it is called Communion Alms and not spent on heat, light, or the minister's salary. Such customs show that the rite is not only a sacrament in the building but a sacrament in the streets. *Liturgy* is Greek for "Work of the people," and this work extends beyond the Church.

"Go forth, you have a mission" is an ingenious mistranslation of *Ite, missa est*, the old words from the end of the medieval Mass, "It is the dismissal." *Missa* does not mean mission, but *missa est* might be stretched to say the end of Mass in the Church is the start of mission in the world.

Four

DO-GOODISM

Caring for Neighbor

This chapter is about the mission that follows the Mass, the thrust of the church into the world after the Lord's Supper. Based on loyalty to God, the mission is to serve these ever more dear United States (or France or India or wherever our citizenship is in this world), to be honest in our work, to bring up good children, to try to be what is covered by that strong but unassuming title "decent folk." At the heart of our mission is caring for neighbor.

It is often laughed at as do-goodism, another putdown that discourages the timid but steadies the tough-minded. The tough-minded know that jokes can only be made about live issues; religion itself isn't safe until it gets into the funny papers. And the tough-minded know further that every side of life suffers ridicule. The honorable term *gothic* was at one time applied contemptuously to the architecture of the Middle Ages as the style of the Goths, rude, barbarous; in the eighteenth century the art of the Counter-Reformation was derided as *baroque* (literally, a misshapen pearl). In politics, taunts are so frequent that every candidate is constantly warned, "If you can't stand the heat, stay out of the kitchen!" None of this bothers the stouthearted in any area of life, as Bunyan's Pilgrim knew:

Who so beset him round
With dismal stories,
Do but themselves confound
His strength the more is.

Caring for others is often put over against being aware of God, the historic contrast of works versus faith, which may seem to divide churchmen into busybodies and dreamers. In practice, however, the apparent division unites them. The Christian's (and Jew's) first and great commandment is to love God (Pentecostalism); his second, equal to the first, is to love his neighbor as himself (do-goodism). No one argues which is first or second as long as both commandments are kept. Churchmen work as well as worship; they build hospitals alongside churches, teach the binomial theorem along with baptism, and struggle for justice while they pray. The Association of Christian Camps in Japan sets standards for sewage disposal along with standards for Bible study. The late Dag Hammarskjöld of the United Nations wrote, "In our era, the road to holiness necessarily passes through the world of action."

Social Cancer

Holiness in the world of action used to be known as the Social Gospel, but the name is now suspect because it became contaminated with unworkable politics and economics. "Social" sounds like "socialism," hence when anyone says "social" anything he takes care to distinguish it from socialism. At least this is true in America, where socialism has two meanings in common speech, one so cancerous it vitiates the good in the other. In the benign sense, as Europeans use the word, socialism stands for helping the underdog; in the malignant sense, it stands for tyranny. Americans remember that Stalin defined socialism as "statistics plus control." He was saying, in effect, get the facts and then compel from the top what has to be done. It was similar total control that slowly dragged down Italian Fascist Socialism and German Nazi Socialism and now shadows the Union of Soviet Socialist Republics and the People's Republic of China. There were similar government tyrannies in the Germany of the Kaisers and the Japan of the Greater East Asia Co-Prosperity Sphere. Although these last two had aristocratic trappings, like the present-day military juntas, they were just as stultifying as the so-called dictatorship of the proletariat. Complete social control is the same whether it leads with the left foot or the right. In the days of the black shirts and brown shirts, a well-traveled missionary bishop said, "Whether the diaper is black, brown, or red, it's the same stink!"

The Communism revived by Lenin-Stalin in this century insisted that you cannot raise the poor and enslaved without first possessing dictatorial power; but never mind, they add, this power will wither away when social justice is finally established. (Besides, you can't make an omelet without breaking eggs.) Present-day Communism is nothing like the communism practiced in the early Church by some of its members (*Acts* 2:44; 4:32), which was entirely voluntary—an expression of the trust they had in one another. It did not succeed, and Paul had to do a lot of money-raising to bail out the brethren who experimented with it (*1 Corinthians* 16:1–3). Later, whenever voluntary communism has reappeared (as in New England's Brook Farm, New York's Oneida Community, or Canada's Universal Brotherhood, Ltd.), it has proved ineffective in practice, however noble in purpose. Modern Communists claim they will escape this ineffectiveness by allying their social theories with tyranny on a vast scale, thus removing the handicap of freedom that had caused the voluntary communes to fail. The result has been fearful human suffering which still has not produced consumer goods; hence free men fight against all tyrannies even though they appreciate their commendable promises. The sad truth is that the democracies have not always worked hard enough to light up the dark places of the world, so some people turn to Communism rather than to democracy as "the last best hope of earth."

The contrast between Soviet control and the free world has been a bitter lesson in the differences between caring for neighbor under tyranny and caring for him under freedom. There are many degrees in between, but whenever caring heads toward the police state it becomes un-Christian because it destroys liberty, an essential element of the Gospel. Believers are suspicious of the growth of bureaucracy in a free society, for they have seen beneficent statisms become oppressive as one government restriction leads to another.

Such fear of regulation can lead to the opposite extreme, the belief that private virtue alone will bring the good life. It will not unless every last person becomes totally good and wise. In the meantime, there has to be legislation to curtail sharp practices, wise laws to hinder the hindrances to the good life. Some measure of coercion has always been present in all social planning, but it stops far short of totalitarian socialism. There is plenty of free space between "Damn you, Jack, I'm all right" (laissez-faire) and "Damn you, Jack, I know best" (socialism). A simple illustration of this free space would be the case of six out of ten manufacturers who as a matter of conscience stop polluting the air. Democracy says those six have the legal right to compel the four others to do what their consciences have not yet told them to do. Otherwise, the four will put the six out of business with the money they save by defiling the environment.

Another illustration of benign social coercion is military life. It provides free dentistry, board, and pension and requires every soldier to obey a hierarchy up to one commander-in-chief. This military socialism is necessary in the fearful emergency of war, yet strangely it is not perceived as socialism, because the very idea is proscribed in the services. Officer candidates of World War II remember the absurd question, "Have you ever had any liberal tendencies?" The soldier's bad experience with the socialism in the Army makes him reject it in civilian life. He thinks he was opposed to militarism, but his real dislike was socialism. He realizes that business under the military is deadening compared to business in private life. (In all fairness, business is not the military's job.) An enthusiastic grocer or schoolteacher dislikes the Army because it stifles initiative: "soldiering" is taking things easy, "regimentation" comes from regimental life. These derivatives result from a bad exposure to socialism. I say this in spite of twenty-seven happy years in the Naval Reserve, where I learned how much private initiative exists in the armed forces, to the great benefit of our country. Nevertheless, in the awful event of war, unquestioning obedience is the bedrock of national self-defense. Herman Wouk's *Caine Mutiny* showed the subtlety of the conflict between initiative and obedience.

Keeping in mind the cancer of tyranny that lurks in total social control, I want to consider examples of the good use of that prickly adjective *social*.

Social Prosperity

In our era, the road to holiness passing through the world of action has to make prosperity its first step. The theme of *Genesis*, the first book of the Bible, is prosperity, which has three synonyms that are repeated over and over in Scripture: wealth, riches, plenteousness. These are commonly associated today with luxury, but in the Bible they represent what we would call an adequate standard of living, or a minimum income, or enough for everybody. The four words are used interchangeably and always with eyes on the poor; prosperity has to be *social*—that is, for all people. "The question of bread for myself is a material question, but the question of bread for my neighbor, for everybody, is a spiritual and religious question," said Nicholas Berdyaev, Eastern Orthodox theologian. It is possible for a community to be poverty-stricken while the top people live comfortably and the head man of a savage tribe always has a silk hat and an umbrella.

The first requisite for helping the bottom people is to *produce more goods;* distributing them comes afterward. It does not always follow, but in any case it has to be second, *after* production. The unexpressed premise of Biblical economics is that before distribution there must be something to distribute, hence the constant prayer for prosperity, wealth, riches, and plenteousness. There follow many stern admonitions in the Bible about a fair sharing of the good things that have been produced. So many admonitions, perhaps, that distribution without more production became one of the heresies of nineteenth-century Christianity. Scholars tell us that this false emphasis may have derived from the British Empire, spread over a quarter of the globe, whose liberal colonizers came down one-sidedly on distributing wealth without seeming to be aware of the need for creating more wealth. Whether or not this overemphasis springs solely from Britain, today's "have-not" nations must rethink the idea that redistribution is their only panacea and begin to promote hard labor. Prosperity is not only for all people but is produced by all people. Inequalities are a matter not so much of birth as of work performance.

The "have" nations furnish what business schools call "case studies for the growth of prosperity," and since religion is one reason for the growth, such studies belong also in theological schools. Both commerce and theology could use the same data. A dramatic case study has been furnished in the past forty years by the island of Puerto Rico.

It was abysmally poor yet moved into relative prosperity within living memory, and the new wealth (Biblical wealth, remember, not luxury) was helped by a religious revival, dogmatics aiding economics.

The island had been Roman Catholic since the first Spanish settlements in the sixteenth century. Political freedom was won at the start of the twentieth century; but the economy remained feudalistic, and the descendants of the colonial aristocracy continued to hold power for another forty years, giving Puerto Rico (Rich Harbor) the ironic title "Poorhouse of the Caribbean." The situation changed just before World War II, when an idealistic American government inaugurated Operation Bootstrap, an economic reform, and at the same time zealous Pentecostal missionaries arrived in the island. Conventional Protestant churches had always been there in small numbers quietly ministering to foreigners, but the new missionaries evangelized the natives by playing the cornet on street corners and putting up neon signs that blinked "Jesus Saves."

The result of their mission was a startling change in the living habits of the very poor. Drinking was cut down, the rum weekend was nearly abolished. On Monday mornings workers were no longer hung over, with trembling hands that ruined expensive machinery in the new factories. Religious proselyting (its most scornful label) also reduced gambling. Cockfighting is picturesque, but workers who gave it up because they were convinced it was sinful now kept their wages for their children's shoes. With new religious enthusiasm a strictness came into sex morality, slums became less like barnyards, there were less stabbings and fewer abandoned children. A by-product of these changes was a dependable working force, from which industrialization could follow fast. The new ethics growing from a faith in God did as much for Operation Bootstrap as was done by enlightened government, fair wages, cellist Pablo Casals, and the good climate for executives advertised by the Puerto Rican Chamber of Commerce.

Puerto Rico is a next-door sample. Many far-off places are also struggling out of poverty, and similar changes are going on. The American government's part in assisting these changes began with President Franklin Roosevelt's Good Neighbor Policy, aimed at Latin America. This sparked Operation Bootstrap through the commissioners he appointed for Puerto Rico. After World War II, President Truman led a massive aid program, known as the Marshall Plan, for the prostrate nations of Europe. Later, under the Point Four Program, technical advisers were sent to other parts of the world. President Eisenhower widened foreign aid to Asia and Africa. President Kennedy increased the emphasis on Latin America by his Alliance for Progress, usually known by its Spanish name, *Alianza para el Progreso*, to highlight the fact that the effort is South American as well as North American.

The billions in public funds, private investments, and technical knowledge that the United States and other rich nations are making available will gradually be exceeded, it is hoped, by the efforts of the nationals of the poor countries. Everything turns on whether they themselves succeed in establishing sufficiently productive economies, a hope expressed by the slogan "Trade, not Aid." Whatever the technology and commerce, aid and trade all over the world are more than factories and farms—they are a new society.

The speeches and editorials keep saying that social prosperity will come only as everyone works harder, taxes fall equitably on rich and poor, schooling and voting are made available, better means are found to limit the population growth, workers get a fair share of profits, native capital stops sneaking abroad, and faltering governments are no longer taken over by the military. One glaring requirement is to do away with the assumption that the *mordida*, or worn-out philosophy of graft, is inevitable in business and government. Today's papers are full of new charges of graft initiated by American firms seeking business in Europe and Asia. It is not clear how widespread the practice is or who began it. But never mind about casting the first stone; all hands must eliminate under-the-counter gifts if only because they block business growth. The foundation for plenteousness is ethics.

That is the reason the ethical thrust of foreign missions has always been important for the spread of the good life. Long before people knew about "have" and "have-not" nations, they knew that the Christian Church carried on a work from haves to have-nots called "taking the Gospel to the heathen." When cynics say that government aid has nothing to do with generosity but is a selfish device for halting the spread of tyranny, they should be contradicted. The aid is largely prompted by care for neighbor, and the neighborhood is the world. The votes against the return of American isolation came in good measure from the sermons on Christian missions heard every third Sunday in worship across the land.

The connection between prosperity and religion has to be stressed, because the evidence is not obvious unless the news is carefully read. The fact is often missed that a prosperous, wealthy, rich, plenteous society must first be a virtuous society. If this view seems naïve, it may be accepted when stated negatively by a sociologist friend, Richard L. Meier: "In various parts of the underdeveloped world the prospects for economic growth will not become particularly bright until there are some rather profound changes in human motivations and values in the sociopolitical structure." This business-school phrase, "rather profound changes in human motivations and values in the sociopolitical structure," would be reduced in the theological seminary to one word: *conversion*. From the beginning, dealing with the Third World keeps lapsing into religious terminology. "We must evangelize them," said the *Alianza's* first superbly successful director, Teodoro Moscoso.

Religion is not the only factor that will bring a decent standard of living to the Third World. There must be tax advantages for new factories, honest auditing, and wise labor regulations so that the gains of hard work do not accrue to only one group. There has to be social morality as well as private morality. But new laws are made possible by new ethics among individuals. Whether good people or good laws come first is another chicken-egg question, but it is certain that a good economic structure does not function without good people. And it was equally certain, said a scholar close to Puerto Rico, that "the Bible ethic provided the staying power of a social reform. It reduced the volatility of a population which otherwise sought immediate gratification of its wants."

While recognizing all these things, we must note that neither Protestants nor Roman Catholics (nor the newcome Pentecostals in Puerto Rico nor Jews nor Muslims, for that matter) would say that factory or farm output is the motive for faith. Social prosperity, like personal health, is a by-product of faith, although neither follows inevitably.

If wealth, prosperity, riches, and plenteousness lose their matrix of faith, they behave in the strange way seen in parts of mainland American life (and very recently in Puerto Rico), where the problems of the irreligious are made worse by a rise in their standard of living. Abolishing physical hunger only clears the way for the hungers of the mind and heart; man really does not live by bread alone. The issue, as some children of modern suburbia think they were the first to discover, is not primarily to make a living, but to make a life, to learn how to be, in a time of material affluence and psychic impoverishment. Materialism is a dead end; an irony that threatens both the developed and the developing nations, and makes the humor of the song in *Oklahoma!*:

Everything's up to date in Kansas City,
They've gone about as far as they can go.

Social Liberty

As holiness passes through the world of action, another
crucial step is toward liberty. This is proclaimed in the
second book of the Bible, describing the exodus out of
Egyptian slavery. "Thus saith the Lord God of Israel, Let
my people go" (*Exodus* 5:1). Freedom is as primary as
prosperity for a good life (and perhaps, as the Irishman
said, both are first). Nations that have put liberty ahead of
economic growth have done better than those that put
tyranny before economic growth. Free enterprise is essential, clean contrary to police-state theory that control comes
before prosperity.

Of course freedom must be social, thrusting downward to
the depressed. Just as the leaders always live more comfortably than the rank and file, so they are always more
free. The Vichy rulers of France in World War II enjoyed
a freedom not shared by French farmers and taxi drivers.
Our generation, which has observed political changes on
every continent, is disillusioned by seeing colonies freed
from foreign rulers only to get native "liberators" more
dictatorial than their former colonialists. The government is
free but the people are not. The Middle Ages had a watch-
word, "freedom of the cities, liberty of the princes," but
what happened to the bottom ninety percent of the population (the peasants) was never mentioned. Today's aim is
prosperity and liberty for all, a chicken in the pot for every
free American and a glass of milk for every free Hottentot,
slogans derived from the Bible, however much they got
batted around in politics.

From first to last, the Bible tells of the fight for freedom.
Freedom's actual history, as distinguished from the legen-

dary, begins in *Exodus* when God freed the Jews, and ends in *Revelation* when God condemned the Beast with 666 on his forehead (the ruling Roman tyrant). In Moses's struggle with Pharaoh, God inflicted ten plagues on Egypt (*Exodus* 7 to 13), the last one being the death of the oldest child in every Egyptian family. On that fearful night, the angel of death spared the Jewish children by passing over their homes (hence the word Passover).

Thirteen hundred years later, a company of Jews were holding their yearly celebration in an upper room at Jerusalem with their leader, Jesus of Nazareth. What he said that night about being the giver of new life applies to politics as well as to religion. Paul relates it to national freedom when he writes, "Christ our Passover is sacrificed for us," as Americans might say, "Christ our Fourth of July is sacrificed for us," the French, "Christ our Bastille Day."

The tie between Christ's resurrection and the Jewish Passover is so close that the Resurrection in many countries is called the Passover (*Pâques, Pascua, Pasqua*). The name *Easter* was brought in by our heathen ancestors. Its changing date each year follows the Passover's shifting date, which was determined by the moon before there were any calendars. The *Exodus* slaves needed a full moon to escape in a night flight. They never forgot which full moon it was —the one after the vernal equinox, when day and night are equal (our March 21). Easter Day, therefore, is always the first Sunday after the full moon after March 21. The yearly annoyance of a shifting holy day is valuable if only as a reminder that liberty is not easily won.

Liberty's immense cost is symbolized by the plagues that broke the will of Egypt's tyrant. Unleavened bread was eaten at Passover because in the hurried escape there was no time to let the bread rise. That frightened haste is preserved in the use of unleavened bread (*matzos*) at modern Jewish rites, and in the Christian Lord's Supper. Jews eat lamb with bitter herbs at their yearly celebration because it

was eaten on that first Passover night; Christians call Jesus
the *Agnus Dei* (Lamb of God). In a fifth-century prayer
Christ is "the very Paschal [Passover] Lamb which was
offered for us," and an eighth-century hymn is still sung:

> The Day of Resurrection
> Earth tell it out abroad,
> The Passover of gladness,
> The Passover of God.

The Jewish Passover antedates Thermopylae, the Magna
Carta, and the Emancipation Proclamation. The victory
gained then has been a golden thread in Jewish and Christian history. Bishops stood with the barons who forced
King John to sign at Runnymede. Five of the seven editors
of the first English *Book of Common Prayer* (1549) were
martyred for reasons that were as political as they were
theological. Their use of the word "common" had a suspi-
ciously levelling sound: were the writers saying that all
men, people and priest, peasant and peer, were equal before God? The very existence of such a book implied the
democratic idea that everyone could learn to read it, as did
the Bibles that Henry VIII had chained in the churches for
the people's use. In the nineteenth century, Sunday schools
were started because there were no weekday schools for the
poor; their original purpose was not to teach religion but
the three R's, which ultimately enfranchised the illiterate.
The Liberty Bell in Philadelphia does not get its name from
July 4, 1776, but from Bible words cast earlier around the
rim: "Proclaim liberty throughout all the land unto all the
inhabitants thereof" (*Leviticus* 25:10).

The innumerable instances of the tie between the Bible
and liberty make strange the question of the 1960s: why
should church people take part in freedom marches? Freedom is their word; they respond to it like old fire horses
smelling smoke. A related question is: why do modern

tyrannies always bring back the anti-Semitism of the old tyrannies? The answer is that Jews are fighters for freedom and are always a menace to tyrants. There were Jewish leaders in the 1917 Communist revolution, but there are few in the Soviet government now, and Jews are being persecuted in the 1970s as they were under the czars.

Readers of the Bible believe that God is the Author of liberty. The deist Thomas Jefferson saw this: "The God who gave us life, gave us liberty"; and the anticlerical Voltaire, when asked to bless Benjamin Franklin's grandson, placed his hand on the child's head and said, "I give you two words, God and Liberty." Freedom is mentioned so often in the drawn-out cold war against the new imperialisms that the word grows stale. It was equally stale in the days when Hitler's tyranny might have been stopped but inaction was excused with slogans like "It isn't necessary to be free Jews; it's necessary to be good Jews." Good Jews are free Jews, and "better red than dead" or "better slave than grave" are sad echoes of "Better for us to serve the Egyptians, than that we should die in the wilderness" (*Exodus* 14:12). In their Passover escape God did not lead the people through "the land of the Philistines, although that was near; for God said, Lest peradventure the people repent when they see war, and they return to Egypt" (*Exodus* 13:17). Although Jews and Christians have had to live under despotisms at times, they have never done so willingly, and their Bible produced menacing songs:

> Go down, Moses,
> Way down to Egyptland;
> Tell old Pharaoh,
> Let my people go.

The spirituals sounded peaceful in the moonlight under the magnolias with banjos strumming, but later they were marched to in dangerous daylight.

Social Ethic of Work

The Bible religions are not only connected with prosperity and liberty, they are also tied to hard work, white-collar as well as blue-collar. The popularizing of this truth goes back to a memorable passage by Montesquieu, who observed that the English "had progressed furthest of all people in three important things: piety, commerce, and freedom." He went on to point out that "the debt of the third of these admirable attributes to the first had often been emphasized. Freedom owes much to piety. Was it possible that the second might also owe something to it? Did commerce also owe much to piety?"

Max Weber, the German scholar, answered yes. He argued that "the connecting link was to be found in the influence of the religious movement whose greatest figure had been Calvin." Weber was saying that Protestantism is the chief cause of prosperity, and he coined the phrase "Protestant Ethic," which was later brought to wide notice by R. H. Tawney's *Religion and the Rise of Capitalism.* Now the cliché is used so widely that people believe that Protestantism is a conspiracy for making people work. As usually employed, Protestant ethic is a putdown like Puritan ethic and Mormon ethic, supposedly a device for deluding people into industriousness. "Those sobersides earn the money; the Quakers dress plainly in gray, but I notice it's always gray silk." To limit a capacity for work to a small segment of the population suggests that it is merely the idiosyncrasy of that particular sect. Work has even been known in a recession as the White House ethic, a presidential device for getting more productivity out of the population.

Protestant ethic is a misnomer; the ethic is also Jewish and Roman Catholic. It is derived from their common book and should be called the Bible ethic. Amintore Fanfani, the Italian statesman, was among many scholars who questioned Weber's adjective "Protestant." When Fanfani was a professor of economics, he argued that Catholicism invented capitalism long before the Reformation and that after it, Roman Catholics pursued business just as energetically as Protestants. But perhaps not quite as energetically, because when Fanfani faced the fact that Protestant countries were wealthier than Roman Catholic ones, he offered the theory that long-headed Northerners make better businessmen than round-headed Southerners. If Protestants do work harder, a more likely reason than head shape is that they were more accustomed than Catholics to reading the Bible until *aggiornamento* (updating) by Pope John XXIII encouraged greater Catholic reading. I reject both ethnic peculiarities and phrenology as causes of industriousness and insist that the material progress of the poor all over the world is being furthered by Jews, Catholics, and Protestants, all teaching their Bible inheritance of hard work.

Work gets more support in the Bible than in any other sacred writings. In the beginning, the creation of the world is pictured as an activity from which God had to take time off. It was the kind of effort tediously called making a buck or meeting a payroll. No matter whether God made the world in six days or six hundred million years, the vital question is whether His task could possibly have compelled Him to rest. Is an alternation of toil and surcease part of ultimate reality? Or is work a punishment for man's disobedience, as Adam was told after he and Eve ate the forbidden fruit? "In the sweat of thy face shalt thou eat bread" (*Genesis* 3:19). If we read past Adam, the Bible reflects the Hebrew delight in laboring men, in cunning artificers, in those who built walls, such as found out musical tunes, and recited verses in writing (*Ecclesiastes* 44:5). Manual effort was necessary to care for the cattle upon a thousand hills and to rebuild Jerusalem; there is no suggestion that these tasks be left to slaves so the religious could meditate.

Every Jewish boy had to learn a trade of hand labor.

However scholarly his principal occupation, he also had to cut wood or plow. Paul, the scholar, may have held up his hands when he said, "These hands have ministered unto my necessities" (*Acts* 20:34) to show they were stained black from the wool of tent-making. Jesus was a carpenter; his first disciples included fishermen and tax gatherers, not drudgery-free intellectuals. The bread and wine of the Lord's Supper are manufactured products; they are wheat and grapes that have been processed into food and drink, not the raw produce shown in church decoration. The first task of Francis of Assisi, when he went beyond nominal Christianity, was to spend two years rebuilding a ruined church by solitary effort. Brother Lawrence, author of *The Practice of the Presence of God*, was a dishwasher. The Shaker Church motto was "Hands to work, hearts to God."

All through history, this Bible emphasis persists. "Earn all you can, save all you can, give all you can" was a teaching of John Wesley that helped make England's industrial revolution peaceful. Without industrious individuals there is no industrial wealth. Neither is there any world peace. Pope Paul VI wrote, "The new name for peace is development." So while care for neighbor leads a Bible reader to coach slum kids on Tuesday night and attend a charity committee at Thursday lunch, it also makes him toil at his regular job Monday through Friday. "People of faith and hope express themselves in creation," wrote Thornton Wilder. "These men and women work. The spectacle that most discourages them is not error or ignorance or cruelty, but sloth."

The Victorians hung wall mottoes in their attic bedrooms: "Servants, obey in all things your masters according to the flesh; not with eye-service, as men-pleasers; but in single-ness of heart, fearing God" (*Colossians* 3:22). Egalitarians who smile knowingly at such attic maxims sometimes have not heard of the needlepoint in the Victorian parlors: "Masters, give unto your servants that which is just and equal;

knowing that ye also have a Master in heaven" (*Colossians* 4:1). The Bible's directives apply both upstairs and downstairs and are needed wherever the ethical climate condones laziness or exploitation. Owners need employees who toil for God's sake, and workers need employers who toil for God's sake. One of the Church's modest tasks in every city and village is to fortify conscientious workers in both white and blue collars. One of its larger tasks is to encourage greater candidness of speech in the United Nations and other world forums, to make plain that underdevelopment is not the result of colonialism but often of laziness.

The ethic of work is a social ethic, but it depends, like every other social good, on private conduct. Owner and worker, joined by the manager, depend on each other's consciences more than on union contracts and government regulations. In the end, there is no bookkeeping by which the three can be checked so completely that cheating is impossible. Or, to put it positively, prosperity comes only as every man is responsible in his daily labor. It is God who wants men to deal truly with each other, and He will require this at their hands. It all goes back to the Bible, whose young readers memorize verses like these:

> Seest thou a man diligent in his business? he shall stand before kings. . . . Yet a little sleep, a little slumber, a little folding of the hands to sleep: So shall thy poverty come as one that travelleth; and thy want as an armed man. (*Proverbs* 22:29; 24:33–34)

> Every man should eat and drink, and enjoy the good of all his labor, it is the gift of God. . . . There is nothing better, than that a man should rejoice in his own works; for that is his portion. (*Ecclesiastes* 3:13, 22)

> Jesus answered them, My Father worketh hitherto, and I work. . . . I must work the works of him that

sent me, while it is day: the night cometh, when no
man can work. (*John* 5:17; 9:4)

In Sunday schools they sing a rollicking tune:

> Work for the night is coming,
>   Work through the morning hours;
> Work while the dew is sparkling,
>   Work 'mid springing flowers.
> Work when the day grows brighter,
>   Work in the glowing sun,
> Work for the night is coming
>   When man's work is done.

Possibly this hymn means the Vineyard of the Lord, but it
also applies to the office or factory where earnest adolescents get their first jobs during school vacations.

Social Grace

If prosperity, liberty, and the work ethic are the first three
names in the Church's social register, grace is the fourth. A
Christian does not excuse his lack of pleasantness on the
ground that he is engaged in good causes. He tries not only
to do good but also to be good to those who work with him,
and to those who live with him. He avoids graceless righteousness, a contradiction not always recognized. The road
to holiness is *pleasant* as it passes through the world of
action. "We liberals are so superior to everything," wrote
Albert Jay Nock, "that we fail in the smaller amenities that
the conservative is strong on. We are so taken up with our
general love of humanity that we don't have time to be
decent to anybody. How can you tell when sauerkraut has
gone sour?"

Social grace is human graciousness and differs from religious grace, which is God's power freely given to man. This second use of the word is a special theological one. Man does not earn this grace but simply accepts it. Grace in this sense is God's Spirit touching man, something man can feel almost physically. The current popularity of the old song is further evidence of the commonness of mysticism:

> Amazing grace, how sweet the sound,
>   That saved a wretch like me,
> I once was lost, but now am found,
>   Was blind, but now I see.

> 'Twas grace that taught my heart to fear,
>   And grace my fears relieved;
> How precious did that grace appear
>   The hour I first believed.

Under social grace I'm not talking about amazing grace but about simple kindness between people. The absence of it explains why many names in philanthropy carry a slight sneer: do-gooder, Lady Bountiful, utopian reformer, social engineer, case worker. "Do you only care about the bleeding crowd? How about the needy friend?" was the one intelligible couplet in the lyrics of a recent rock musical. "My son, blemish not thy good deeds, neither use uncomfortable words when thou givest any thing. Shall not the dew assuage the heat? so is a word better than a gift. Lo, is not a word better than a gift? but both are with a gracious man" (*Ecclesiasticus* 18:15–17). "The grace of our Lord Jesus Christ" (*Romans* 16:20) meant his surprising charm. "All... wondered at the gracious words which proceeded out of his mouth" (*Luke* 4:22). "Never man spake like this man" (*John* 7:46).

The Apostle Paul in *1 Corinthians* 13:1–3 made inner attitudes more important than outward actions. A paraphrase of it might read, "Though I make eloquent and moving social pronouncements, and have not love, I am become as sounding brass or a tinkling cymbal . . . and though I bestow all my goods to feed the poor, and though I give my body to be clubbed in demonstrations, and have not love, it profiteth me nothing." The Greek word Paul uses here for love is *agape*, whose depth of meaning in Christianity cannot be exaggerated. But long before Christ, in Homeric Greek, it meant simply giving salt and bread to a stranger, and however it has been deepened to include the profoundest love, *agape* has never lost its original meaning of elementary courtesy.

It is surprising to realize how much time Jesus devoted to manners. "When thou art bidden of any man to a wedding, sit not down in the highest room" (*Luke* 14:8); "Let your communication be Yea, yea; Nay, nay" (*Matthew* 5:37); "Eat such things as are set before you. . . . Go not from house to house" (*Luke* 10:8, 7); "Friend, how camest thou in hither not having a wedding garment?" (*Matthew* 22:12); "Beware of the scribes, which love to go in long clothing, and love salutations in the marketplaces" (*Mark* 12:38); "When thou doest alms, let not thy left hand know what thy right hand doeth" (*Matthew* 6:3). Whatever happened at the wedding in Cana of Galilee when Jesus turned the water into wine, it was a miracle of simple kindness, and John counts it the beginning of miracles, which made his disciples believe on him (*John* 2:11). The healing of the sick boy, which followed, John carefully lists as "the second miracle that Jesus did" (*John* 4:54). First, politeness; second, healing the body.

"Manners maketh man" was the motto of William of Wykeham, the leading educator of fourteenth-century England, founder of New College, Oxford, and Winchester School. Politeness is sometimes superficial polish, but it is often the steady discipline in kindness that gradually turns into caring for neighbor. Ultimately it goes back to faith, as the shrewd novelist Honoré Balzac, knew: "True courtesy

implies Christian thinking, it is like the flower of charity."
Agreeable strangers are not necessarily riverboat gamblers;
they could be kind souls who have overcome their natural
shyness, and obedient to the old maxim *memento vivere*,
"remember to live," they spread good by their bearing as
well as by their checkbooks and committees. When Pope
John XXIII received a delegation of Jews who needed his
help, his greeting to them was, "I am Joseph, your brother."
The grace of this tender welcome comes from the story of
Joseph and his brothers (*Genesis* 42 to 45).

Politeness has an important place also in evangelism, the
most beautiful word to have fallen on evil days. Think of
the courses that used to be given at religious conferences on
how to approach strangers on railroad trains! Who has the
right to so invade another's life? What busybodies hide behind the lovely old phrase "personal witness"! Yet when
asked, believers today are as eager to respond to strangers
on buses and planes as Bunyan's Evangelist was when Pilgrim broke out with "a great and lamentable cry: 'What
shall I do?' "

Desperately needed spiritual help is governed by *agape*.
Believers seldom mention their faith unless requested, nor
do they lead around to it by circumlocutions. With these
two negatives goes a frightening positive: believers, if
asked about their faith, must be ready to speak out, loud
and clear, even when sometimes the asking is no more than
a hint. The sharpest regret comes from having had no help
to give when it was sought. Do-gooders are annoying, but
those who wish they could do good and cannot are tragic.
"Be ready always to give an answer to every man that ask-
eth you a reason of the hope that is in you with meekness
and fear" (*1 Peter* 3:15).

A new appreciation of grace is shown by the use of the
word *charisma* in politics (*Charis* is Greek for "grace.")
Candidates for public office are said to be born with it; but
it is more likely that charisma is acquired by education.

Through training, a child can be taught courtesy and consideration, pleasantness of dress and voice. Such schooling is important in a democracy, where people should not be limited by early environment but allowed to develop their potentialities. In her bequest for improving the manners of the Irish, Mrs. George Bernard Shaw wrote, "Human nature is corrigible," and the Apostle Paul insisted that a loving disposition could be acquired. That he was not born with one is shown by several ill-tempered passages in his letters. Words like these are written out of hard self-discipline:

> This love of which I speak is slow to lose patience—it looks for a way of being constructive. It is not possessive; it is neither anxious to impress nor does it cherish inflated ideas of its own importance. Love has good manners and does not pursue selfish advantage. It is not touchy. It does not keep account of evil or gloat over the wickedness of other people. On the contrary, it is glad with all good men when truth prevails. (*1 Corinthians* 13:4–6)

"How unlike the conventional reformer John Woolman was," wrote Dean Willard Sperry of Harvard about the Quaker of colonial New Jersey:

> The unwillingness to blame even those of whose conduct he could not approve, the determination not to be drawn into hasty words of which he would repent or betrayed into tedious words which had become mechanical formulas, the resolution that his concern must be new every morning with something of its first freshness, the refusal to force the pace of events beyond present possibility, the historical patience which was content to bide God's time—from all these traits

the modern advocate of the social gospel has much to learn.

Social Progress

In 1772 Woolman noted in his *Journal,* "I have gone forward, not as one travelling in a road cast up, and well prepared, but as a man walking through a miry place, in which are stones here and there, safe to step on: but so situated that one step being taken, time is necessary to see where to step next."

The complexity of social progress was made clear to Americans of this generation by theologians like Reinhold Niebuhr who shook the Church from another nineteenth-century heresy, that progress is inevitable. This optimistic theory is expressly denied in the Bible by its many evidences that civilization can also go backward. Each victory for progress brings fresh difficulty on a higher level. Consequently, whenever there is a victory, another struggle looms ahead. The perfect social order will never come in this world even though we are commanded to labor toward it. See the parables of the Wheat and Tares (*Matthew* 13:24–30) and the Good and Bad Fish (*Matthew* 13:47–50). The abolitionists were wrong who thought that ending slavery would settle every evil. The anticolonialists were wrong who thought abolishing empires would end world problems; a study of newly independent African states bears the disillusioned title *The Morning After.* Even a hymn, "Thy Kingdom Come!," is unbiblical because it promises that someday there will be perfect righteousness on earth:

> The day in whose clear-shining light
> All wrong shall stand revealed,

When justice shall be throned in might,
  And every hurt be healed.

When knowledge, hand in hand with peace,
  Shall walk the earth abroad;
The day of perfect righteousness,
  The promised day of God.

No such day is promised in the New Testament this side of eternity except in man's heart; heaven on earth is inner peace in the midst of conflict for progress. The Old Testament poetry about watchmen waiting for the dawn warns that night will come again. Isaiah's exact words were, "Watchman, what of the night? . . . The watchman said, the morning cometh, and also the night" (*Isaiah* 21:11–12). The reason "utopian scheme" has become a scornful phrase is that visionaries often believe their particular reform will bring such a perfect society that no further effort will be needed; indeed they believe their reform to be so final that it justifies any measures to enforce it. Because of such dangerous obsession, the fight for freedom is often flesh and blood defending itself against utopias, religious and political.

The Pre-Raphaelite artists and writers of Queen Victoria's day used the Holy Grail as the symbol of the utopia they were searching for. Max Beerbohm, the writer, drew a caricature of one of them, Dante Gabriel Rossetti, standing on a scaffold in the Oxford Union painting murals of the Arthurian Grail as the formidable Master of Balliol College, Benjamin Jowett, peers up to inquire, "What were they going to do with the Grail when they found it, Mr. Rossetti?"

The Biblical insight on social progress explains why the Supreme Court's desegregation order in 1954 did not bring a utopia to end all racial injustice. That year was a dawn in black history, which was followed, in Isaiah's metaphor, by another night, a pattern well understood at the time by the president of the National Association for the Advancement of Colored People: "There will be cold beer and double-headers with the Yankees but also tedium, mortgages, and taxes. The Negro will discover what the white man knows. It won't be heaven." A century before, his freedom from slavery was a stunning victory for the Negro, but it brought him without adequate training into the hardship of responsibility.

I have a puzzleheaded friend who wonders whether being imported as a slave to America may not have been something of a victory for the black, at least better than being left as a slave in Africa, or neglected as a free savage. He points out that slaves sold to the traders were treated more humanely by Americans than they had been treated by their fellow Africans, and therefore, in the long run, it was some social progress for Negroes when they came to America in the slave ships. The senior Arthur Schlesinger advanced this thesis forty years ago: "On balance, the bondsmen were better fed, clothed and sheltered, and led easier and probably healthier lives than if they had remained in Africa." Professor Schlesinger's judgment aroused no great stir in 1937 when it was published, but recent scholarly books have brought controversy on the same baffling issue. It is clear that the heinous wrong was the slaves' loss of liberty, which nothing can condone. It could only be righted by emancipation, then partial education, next full education in theory, then full education in practice, and finally total equality of opportunity in an integrated society. The last two have not yet come. A far better thing than bringing slavery to the Western hemisphere would have been to stamp it out long ago in Africa, as missionaries like David Livingstone pleaded for at the time. Enlightened imperialists did abolish it in their colonies, but isolationists washed their hands of it for another century.

The slowness of progress can be the subject of stale argument and an excuse for social inaction, whereas its real importance is in re-affirming the Christian theory of progress, which is that new struggles will be necessary after every victory because utopia is a mirage. Those discouraged because the task appears never-ending can take heart from Jesus's "Sufficient unto the day is the evil thereof" (*Matthew* 6:34). He is not telling us to give up, but urging us to do what we can this day; and leave tomorrow to God. We don't have to see the end, but we have to be counted at the beginning.

The far goal is complete equality for the black in America, which will be achieved through a combination of his own efforts and wise laws, and by plodding along day by day facing each day's hazards as they arise. Dangers were present at the start when Lincoln signed the Emancipation Proclamation. At that time he warned us that we only had our harpoon in the whale but now must come years of careful steering or "the beast will destroy us with one flip of its tail."

Throughout this long struggle, the putdown was always present. In the Civil War, a young white officer named Robert Gould Shaw led Negro troops against the South. In a fierce engagement they were wiped out, and the bodies of white officers and black troops were dumped into a common grave. Naturally, feelings ran high. His detractors said of Colonel Shaw, "Let him lie there with his niggers." Years later, when the monument to him was erected on Boston Common, his mother was asked if she wanted the body of her son brought back and buried under it. She paused and said quietly, "No, let him lie there with his niggers." The sneer had become the boast of that valiant woman.

If this view of social progress as victories followed by more battles seems elementary, we remember that a great Roman Catholic lay theologian, Baron Friedrich von Hügel, said the truth comes in three forms: solid, liquid, and gaseous. Parish priests like me use the gaseous form, which we get from the liquid of the scholars; (the solid truth, von Hügel used to say, was for archangels in retreat). Here is a liquid comment on victories and new battles from another scholar, Alfred North Whitehead:

> The final introduction of a reform does not necessarily prove the moral superiority of the reforming generation. . . . A great idea is not to be conceived as merely waiting for enough good men to carry it into practical effect. That is a childish view of the history of ideas. The ideal in the background is promoting the gradual growth of the requisite communal customs adequate to sustain the load of its exemplification.

Whitehead's liquid truth is understood by gaseous questions: Can war be abolished until world government begins to have military power? Can welfare be extended until we have more productivity and can afford more taxes? Could the Supreme Court's 1954 decision have come any earlier? The quick answer in each case is no; a framework has to be built before the ideal in the background can be sustained. In the Roman Empire when abolishing slavery was first advocated, there did not exist at that time "the requisite communal customs adequate to sustain the load of its exemplification." If Rome had abolished slavery when the idea was first proposed, the empire would have collapsed four hundred years earlier. Whitehead continues:

> It may be better that the heavens should fall, but it is folly to ignore the fact that they will fall. Suppose that, in the middle of the nineteenth century, the shock that overwhelmed the Confederate States in the American Civil War had equally overwhelmed the whole of North America and the whole of Europe. The sole hope of progressive civilization would have been lost.

We may speculate about a recovery, but of that we know nothing.

To keep the heavens from falling, social progress may come swiftly in some times but must come slowly in others, depending on the requisite communal customs. It is a childish view of ideas to suppose that reform is merely waiting for enough good men to carry it into practical effect. Pace is the problem, as the Supreme Court recognized by calling for "deliberate speed." When to hurry and when to go slowly are the hard questions, recognizing all the possibilities for self-deception by the unconcerned. The Justices might have quoted more of Francis Thompson's poem *The Hound of Heaven* (Who is God Himself, the Author of social progress) moving

> With unhurrying chase,
> And unperturbèd pace,
> Deliberate speed, majestic instancy.

Social Security

Social security has two meanings, the care society takes of its broken-winged, and society's stability as a body capable of functioning. The first meaning is the common one; it crowds out the second, which too often is taken for granted. Yet corporate existence must be maintained while the never-ending struggle for progress goes on. The heavens can fall if advance is interrupted by continuing turmoil, here or overseas. "Law and order" is another political football. But its advocates are justified in pointing out that social progress is not inevitable, that whole commonwealths can go down. Prosperity and liberty are the fruits of slow growth in a stable society.

Walter Lippmann wrote:

To perpetuate the Republic in this epoch of war and revolution, it is now more than ever necessary that we maintain the marriage of Jeffersonian liberty and Hamiltonian authority. We can do ourselves no greater injury than to become unconscious of either principle; so enamored of freedom that we do not construct strong lawful authority to contain it and sustain it, or so apprehensive of freedom that we seek to deny it and suppress it. The conflict of the two principles can be resolved only by uniting them. Neither can live alone.

My mind does not take in the arguments of politicians, economists, and military leaders over the tension between progress and security until I return to the shipwrecked company on a desert island. Among the survivors there will be a few who cannot bear their share of the pioneering— the wounded, the sick, the insane, and the old—so the able-bodied must provide for them. This is the first meaning of social security as commonly understood. Yet circumstances may arise that make caring for the helpless impossible without jeopardizing the safety of all. When Captain Oates in Scott's Antarctic expedition became too ill to keep up with his companions, he walked off into the blizzard so the expedition would not founder trying to save him. The dilemma of whether to leave or to stay must have been heartbreaking for him, and certainly was for his friends when they discovered what he had done.

The worst tragedy of the desert island would be for a half-starving mob to break into the storehouse and eat up all the food in one night. In lifeboats, such a possibility has to be restrained by revolvers when food and water are low. In developed countries that have universal suffrage, the danger is more complex but just as real. By voting, a majority can establish social services that lead the economy into eventual bankruptcy. Some of the Founding Fathers of America saw long ago what they called the "great beast" destroying social security with votes. "Spend and spend; elect and elect" was a recent cynicism that updated their forebodings.

Isolationists warn that America is so committed to defending the freedom of smaller nations that she is overextended around the world. At the same time, she is so blind to hidden military dangers that she is not spending enough on her own self-defense. If they are right, the combination of concern for neighbor and lack of vigilance will end her existence as a free nation. But if her national existence is secure, there can be no limits to generosity from the Christian point of view. The compulsion is absolute: "I was an hungered, and ye gave me meat; I was thirsty, and ye gave me drink . . . sick . . . in prison" (*Matthew* 25:35–36).

The command to help in the bleak areas at home is also absolute. The question asked of Jesus, "Who is my neighbor?" he answered by another question, "Which now of these three, thinkest thou, was neighbor unto him that fell among the thieves?" (*Luke* 10:36). Yet as both foreign aid and domestic welfare increase in cost, they have to be balanced against the economic stability of the nation. Charity will stop cold in a bankrupt state; generosity and prudence are twin Christian virtues. A husband will give a dollar to a beggar who catches him answering the doorbell; his wife, from more experience, may refuse. The husband does not realize how many more beggars will come when the news of the handout gets around, and she has the children's school lunches to pay for. This difference does not prove that women are less warmhearted than men and therefore should be ruled by them (as one theologian opined before the Women's Liberation movement began). Rather it demonstrates how the heart must push the head into more care for the helpless, while the head must push the heart into better management of resources. Although Hippocrates discovered 2,400 years ago that heart and head are the same thing, we use the convention to convey the struggle in the one organ between kindness and practicality. And being in the heart business myself and knowing how hard it is to "conciliate, appease, soften the hearts of angry men," I am content in the head business to follow the aforesaid politicians, economists, and military leaders.

Applying both kindness and practicality to helping the underprivileged nations is again what the Church calls mission and the Government calls foreign aid. Neither the Church nor the Government is proposing that we destroy ourselves in the effort to save every last person. Christian theory has never implied that if only we divided all our wealth, everyone in the world would have enough (that was British Socialism, 1890–1950). The glass of milk for every Hottentot could not possibly be paid for out of our present resources, but if we and the Hottentots both work harder to increase productivity and if Americans live more simply, someday the Hottentots can buy their own milk. The task is better management as well as more generosity. In the present disenchantment with aid, few concerned observers question the obligation of the strong to bear the infirmities of the weak (*Romans* 15:1) but only their efficiency in doing it.

Skill is also required to work out better plans for the needy at home. The chicken in every American pot is as hard to produce as the Hottentot glass of milk. The pressing need is not for more money to spend on relief but for better use of the money. Chiselers on the welfare rolls are a menace to many communities. And although it is better to suffer fakers than to starve the needy, it sometimes requires detectives to discover which is which. The problems are so complex that every bipartisan effort to overhaul the entire welfare system is halted by the bewilderment of both conservatives and liberals. Our existing social science cannot explain what is going on; it must learn more before it can move ahead. Do-goodism is an especially shrewd putdown;

it implies that you think you are doing good but don't know how.

To admit some areas of ignorance does not excuse the people who abandon the sociological and economic situations by saying things are just too baffling. Such people are saying they won't play the game unless it is changed before they get into it. The name of the game is social progress; people play it by doing the best they can in the worst of times. Those playing it welcome criticism while they insist on security, two horses hard to drive in a team as Daniel P. Moynihan points out:

> To protect dissent, no matter how noxious, is one thing. To be indifferent to its growth is another. Men who would undo the system may speak, but they must be answered. The less than soul-stirring belief of the liberal in due process, in restraint, in the rule of law is something more than a bourgeois *apparat:* it invokes, I argue, the most profound perception of the nature of human society that has yet been achieved, and, precisely in its acknowledgement of the frailty of man and the persistence of sin and failure, it is in the deepest harmony with the central tradition of Judeo-Christian theology.

The Bible makes clear that social security has the double role of helping the helpless and stabilizing society at the same time. An instance of the dual role is the Fifth Commandment, which relates survival to kindness. "Honor thy father and thy mother: that thy days may be long upon the land which the Lord thy God giveth thee" (*Exodus* 20:12). Honor means not only being polite to parents but providing for them. (In backward countries, children are the only social security of the old, which is one reason for overpopulation.) And father and mother includes grandparents, siblings, cousins, and finally anyone who is helpless. The commandment might even be stretched to include conservation of natural resources and endangered species. The reward for observing this commandment is "that thy days may be long upon the land." On our obedience depends our very survival on earth. It is called "the commandment with promise" (*Ephesians* 6:2). Sociologists would say the promise is persistence potential; or put negatively, indifference to people and nature leads to racial extinction.

A team of Johns Hopkins physicians corroborated this scriptural insight by research which showed that churchgoers (presumably Fifth Commandment keepers) live longer than other people. They jokingly dubbed their discovery the Leo Durocher Syndrome, "nice guys finish last." Of course, Leo the Lip meant just the opposite, that nice guys finish last in the baseball league. The doctors pretended they thought his words meant nice guys last longer in the land, as the Fifth Commandment promised, and as their studies seemed to prove.

Social Organization

Caring for neighbor, like mysticism, is bristling with difficulties. The complexity of the legal, medical, and economic ethics facing social care today could be discouraging. Instead, it's actually encouraging; it shows that progress is going on.

Added to this necessary confusion, a common question harasses the conscientious: which is more important, social or personal ethics? The answer is neither; social and personal include each other, and a Christian's duty is double: "Pure religion and undefiled before God and the Father is this, To visit the fatherless and widows in their affliction, and to keep himself unspotted from the world" (*James* 1:27). So close are social and personal ethics that they are often taken for each other. "Be sure your sin will find you out" is commonly applied to private sins like adultery and embezzlement, but it first referred to pacifism, which is a sin against society. "If ye will go armed before the Lord to war . . . until he hath driven out his enemies . . . ye shall . . . be guiltless. . . . But if ye will not do so, behold, ye have sinned against the Lord; and be sure your sin will find you out" (*Numbers* 32:20–23). By a similar reversal, the favorite text for group morality, "Am I my brother's keeper?" (*Genesis* 4:9), referred originally to a private murder.

Many other instances of mixing texts show that social and private morality belong together. It is fatal to try to separate them, as when Christians conscientious in their personal lives are indifferent to politics and charity, or when political activists lack private virtue. Ethical inconsistency is often mentioned sadly in the Bible: "Israel doth not know, my people doth not consider" (*Isaiah* 1:3). "They have a zeal of God, but not according to knowledge" (*Romans* 10:2).

Besides being separated by ignorance, social and private morality can be separated by cynicism. According to police state theory, private ethics may be the enemy of social progress; hence, goes the argument, lying, stealing, and kidnapping are at times necessary. Sexual immorality seduces young men and women into extremism of the right or the left by transient affairs more than by principles; photographers record a fair amount of hanky-panky in demonstrations. Utopianism gets its bad name precisely here when it excuses private wrong to advance public causes. On this principle, or lack of it, a noted professor declares he knows what is right and wrong for his country but not what is right and wrong for his students.

Good causes depend on good people and good people must have good organization for social reform. The staggering number of community enterprises receiving voluntary support in the United States was first pointed out by Alexis de Tocqueville in 1835 and re-emphasized by another Frenchman, André Siegfried, in 1935. The ability of Americans to organize for good works is important, for history teaches the sad failure of the elite in many older countries to unite for usefulness to their societies. The ruling families of Europe and Asia held privileges for centuries as reward for some ancestor's service long before. The inheritors of power gave less and less in return and, beginning with France in 1789, were gradually swept away. The top people of a modern democracy, quite unlike the bloodline rulers of old autocracies, work hard. And top goes a long way down; a democracy's "nobility" are more numerous and often work harder than the "peasants."

Conscientious people realize that unless they organize, upstart tyrants will organize for them. Hence far-seeing citizens are joining political parties as believers are joining churches. Once delivered from private-mindedness and granted public souls, they become regular Democrats or Republicans and denominational Christians, no matter that "regular" and "denominational" are pejorative labels. In the immediate future, political work at ward and precinct levels may be the important duty for Christians. Too many of them have neglected the established parties and have left the engineering of politics to what the novel *1984* called "bellyfeel"—that is, dreaming of progress instead of undertaking the caucusing, telephoning, and doorbell-pushing that make progress possible. Such efforts are what Whitehead called "promoting the gradual growth of the requisite communal customs adequate to sustain the load." In ancient Israel, a book like *Deuteronomy* provided the customs adequate to sustain the ideals of Isaiah and Jeremiah. Is it significant that after *Genesis* (prosperity) and *Exodus* (liberty), the third book in the Bible is *Leviticus* (organization)?

Organized or private, social or personal, ethics cannot be separated. Even "gay liberation" cannot logically maintain its claim to be a purely private matter. Two hundred years before Christ, a group of Jewish intellectuals concluded that homosexuality was the cause of Sodom's destruction by fire and brimstone. (The Emperor Justinian added that it also caused earthquakes.) Their conclusions were based on *Genesis* 19, in which the men of Sodom demanded to "know" the male strangers Lot was entertaining. The word *sodomy* is derived from this interpretation. But Ezekiel, the prophet, had suggested earlier that the destruction resulted not from personal, but from social sin: "Behold, this was the iniquity of thy sister Sodom, pride, fulness of bread, and abundance of idleness was in her and in her daughters, neither did she strengthen the hand of the poor and needy" (*Ezekiel* 16:49).

Ezekiel's opinion has been corroborated by later rabbinic authorities, by Martin Luther, and by recent students. They point out that the Hebrew word *yadoa*, "to know," implies carnal knowledge in only ten out of the nearly one thousand instances in the Old Testament, and in those ten it always refers to heterosexual relations. Furthermore, Sodom is never mentioned in any Bible passages condemning homosexuality. So perhaps sodomy is not what dictionaries and law books have said it is for 2,200 years, but what Ezekiel said it was 3,000 years ago. It is not personal at all, but social. Or maybe it is both.

Five

SECTARIANISM

Thinking Out Our Faith

Whatever sodomy stands for, the destruction of Sodom by fire and brimstone stands for the downfall of a civilization. It dramatizes Oswald Spengler's *Decline of the West*, Edward Gibbon's *Decline and Fall of the Roman Empire*, Albert Speer's *Inside the Third Reich*, and Arnold Toynbee's *Study of History*, in which twenty-one civilizations go down. Even if the books themselves are seldom read, references to their mournful conclusions are widely circulated. Just to mention decline can turn a whole evening into disputation. Nations and cultures decay just as individuals and families do. Islam once stretched from India to Spain; Spain and Portugal owned half of the Americas; and only yesterday the ghost of the Roman Empire was called up by Mussolini. In the 1980s, while Europe and America may be going down, Africa and Asia may be coming up, confounding Spengler's 1914 prophecy (in his *Decline*) that China and Egypt would never again influence the world!

Such ups and downs in nations are caused by conduct, which in turn depends on religion. Justinian's theory that sodomy produces earthquakes is not scientific, but there is scientific evidence that different morals inexorably produce different results over the decades. The mills of the gods grind slowly, but they grind exceedingly fine. American government and business people returning from abroad are asked about the religions they've seen. What influence do they have on life? How do they shape community standards? Never mind that the Muslims worship on Friday, Jews on Saturday, and Christians on Sunday; what happens Monday through Thursday? Apart from what is done inside their buildings, what do the different religions require on the streets? Is it pretty much the same? Are the Buddhists in South Asia like the Christians in South Dakota except for the interesting figurines you brought home? Between Arabs and Jews in the Middle East, does a difference in religions produce any difference in living conditions? To ask such questions raises the specter of sectarianism, a disparaging name for the very necessary practice of thinking out our faith. Of all putdowns, sectarianism especially lends itself to humor, but the humor boomerangs because it implies that no one has the thinking capacity to work out final answers, that we are at the mercy of our feelings and early playpen conditionings. The dismal conclusion is that logic does not apply to living, or at least we haven't the ability to apply it. The joke is on us.

Hinduism

C. S. Lewis, the Oxford and Cambridge don who enlightened a generation by changing solid into liquid truth in his writings, and then turned liquid into gaseous truth on television, believed that in religion today the only live options are Christianity and Hinduism. Their theoretical differences cause enormous practical consequences:

1. Hinduism believes in reincarnation—that is, that every life returns to this earth after death, in another body. Thus a cat may become a banker, a farmer a monkey, a plumber a ballerina. This rebirth is automatic and does not depend on one's present conduct.

Christianity believes that immortality is entrance into another world and that that world depends upon character.

One of the immediate consequences of the Hindu belief in reincarnation is the armies of useless cattle and monkeys that are an offense to hygiene and economics. They are endured because animals could be reborn human beings and yonder cow might be your great aunt, a bewildering theory to foreign readers and tourists and yet held by millions in Asia. Although the theory is intriguing, its final effect on the believer is depressing. Westerners do not realize this gloomy psychological consequence, because they understand reincarnation with two Christian modifications. One is that those who do well in their present life will be reborn to a better life, but strict Hinduism denies this and insists that the circumstances of rebirth are pure accident and bear no relation to virtue. At rebirth a queen may become a cockroach for no reason except that the wheel of life (a national symbol on the flag of India) is going round and round inexorably, and since everyone is on it, he is bound sometimes to be up and sometimes down. The other modification of reincarnation that makes it less offensive is that Christians think each person retains his identity in successive rebirths: he sometimes remembers his former lives (startling instances are cited), he keeps skills acquired in previous existences (how, otherwise, explain infant prodigies?). In brief, a man's personality is his own. Orthodox Hindus do not believe this at all; they say that what survives is life energy, not personalities. Biologically speaking, people are super-vegetables, mere centers of continuing vitality, sans memory, sans skill, sans personality. As the implication of this is fully grasped, it becomes another peppercorn of meaninglessness.

2. Hinduism believes the physical world is unreal; if you turn around fast enough there won't be anything there. Christianity, on the contrary, is thoroughly materialistic:

> This world's no blot for us,
> Nor blank—it means intensely, and means good;
> To find its meaning is my meat and drink.
> —*Robert Browning*

The antimaterialism of Hinduism is one cause of a caste system that has persisted for over five thousand years and even now is attacked more by the agnostics of Asia than by the religious. When Shaw's *Pygmalion* (the original of *My Fair Lady*) was staged in New Delhi, progressive Indians pointed out bitterly that a Hindu version would be unthinkable. The Cockney flower girl would be an untouchable and never allowed inside the house of Brahmin Henry Higgins. Hindus excuse such rigid social distinctions by saying, "It is not a real world, what does it matter?" Forty centuries of Hinduism in India did nothing to shrink the gap between maharaja and peasant. Whatever progress has been made was due first to British colonialism, later to Mahatma Gandhi and the Congress Party, and now to the fear of Communism. The callousness of rulers until recently has been a persistent fact of their politics, which springs directly from their religion.

The slow pace of social progress under Hinduism comes also from the doctrine that meditation is superior to action, since the world of action is illusory. A Hindu is like a devout member of the family who does not pay his bills on time and cannot boil water but reminds us of Something Important. Yet this deep talent for the spiritual is not matched by the intellect and conscience that likewise come from God. Hinduism is the historic illustration of the danger of mysticism by itself. Christians and Jews argue from the Bible, and Muslims from their Koran, that God made men's bodies for a purpose. He has no interest in seeing them on beds of spikes or offered as living sacrifices to bedbugs, exaggerations that highlight the futilities of

Hindu asceticism. Of course, all religions have fanatical ascetics, but Hinduism presents the paradox of fantastic self-denial (vegetarianism is one of its milder tenets) combined with the sensuality of child marriage and temple prostitution.

Hinduism transplanted to America has attracted followers with the challenge, "Wouldn't it be wonderful to drift into the exalted reveries of Asian sages?" The reply is: "Yes, if the right hand were building schools and the left hand were spreading fertilizer." The final results in Asia are not wonderful; life is a penalty and pessimism is the cloud that hangs over everything. This gloom has not been exported to America. Visiting yogis, holding meditations in hotel ballrooms, startle earnest ladies off their gilt chairs by the possibility of a direct leap into the Unknown, and gurus fascinate rock musicians and transcendentally minded folk. The result is the same here as in Asia, that the devotees often feel excused from thinking and working, on the ground that faith is a drift into Nothingness. They meditate on *Om*, a syllable deliberately chosen for its meaninglessness; or they focus on their navel or chin. They chant *Hare Krishna, Hare Rama* mindlessly, a self-erosion that beats one message on the mind: "Dissolve! Be absorbed!"

The Christian opposite is described by the late Dorothy Sayers, a theologian as well as a detective-story writer, "God does not . . . desire the absorption of the many in the One. His love is anxiously directed to confirm each individual soul in its own identity, so that, the nearer it draws to Him, the more truly it becomes its unique and personal self."

We must note in fairness the good that Hindu abstraction has brought to America. If nothing else, it pushes Christian prayer beyond "Now I lay me down to sleep." Transcendental meditation is becoming so well known that its abbreviation is almost a password: "Are you into TM?" People who are in it remark naïvely that fifteen minutes' meditation before dinner is better than a martini. True, and if Hinduism teaches them discipline in praying, their lives will be enriched. Worship has a joy that grows with practice, wherever it is first learned.

Reincarnation and denial of the physical world are two intellectually subtle concepts that most of the Hindu population does not understand. The uneducated masses are reduced to an amoral belief in many gods, the educated to an irresponsible mysticism. This gulf between unethical polytheism and tolerant spiritualism causes the conflicting life styles in Hinduism. All classes are weakened when different levels of society practice what seems to be the same faith in totally different ways. Elitism is a danger signal in religion. American Christianity may not always succeed in getting professors and teamsters into the same buildings, but it keeps trying and is unhappy with one-type congregations. In pre-Civil War churches, where the galleries were reserved for slaves, the interesting point is not that whites and blacks were seated separately, but that they were expected to understand the same sermons. Today no thoughtful clergyman will accept a call to a parish unless it is a cross section of people or unless he can hope to make it into one. Rufus Jones used to say that Quaker leaders were concerned that 90% of their church members were college graduates.

Criticism of Hinduism, or of any other religion, is rebuked by a character of Thornton Wilder's who "never employed irony and did not understand it, nor was he prepared to view with detachment those beliefs with which so many millions of men had consoled or tormented themselves . . . These were not smiling matters." Trying to avoid irony or detachment, it can be said the West needs mysticism and the East needs involvement, the complementing strengths of Pentecostalism and Do-Goodism. Neither is enough by itself; mind and body are interdependent, theology and technology are companion studies, the world is sacramental. Again and again since the ice age, ideas have saved our bodies by the skin of our teeth as Wilder showed in his play of that name.

Buddhism

Buddhism was a reform movement in Hinduism begun five hundred years before Christ by one of the world's great saints, Siddhartha Gautama. Buddha is his title meaning the Enlightened, as Christ is Jesus' title meaning the Messiah. While Buddha was still a young man, he left wife, children and a life of luxury to seek salvation. Being a devout Hindu he tried the three traditional Hindu paths: asceticism, meditation and charity. (Uncharitable note: charity in Hinduism is not an absolute obligation as it is in the Bible and the Koran but is undertaken for self-culture.) Each of these three paths seemed futile to Buddha, and he came to the conclusion that existence itself is the reason for misery. As a Hindu he believed in both reincarnation and the unreality of the world, and he felt the dreariness of going on with these forever. Finally, sitting one day under a bo tree, he had his great illumination—that desire is the cause of rebirth. If a man could give up all desires he would never be reborn; therefore he would cease to exist. He would pass into Nirvana as a candle flame is blown out. Nirvana means extinction, although it is often mistaken by Westerners as another name for heaven. There is neither heaven nor God in Buddhism; only final nothingness for those fortunate enough to attain total indifference.

Buddha taught for forty years, long enough to describe life's futilities in sickening detail, twenty-five centuries before the same was done by today's novels of despair and our theater of the absurd. The Buddhist scriptures are source books in disillusionment more terrifying than any twentieth-century writings. They counsel man to abandon every longing, bad or good, since existence can give no lasting satisfactions in any direction. Buddha purified the fantastic accumulations of age-old Hinduism by one simple message: give up all desire, and you will be dead forever. (Suicide will not do it, because suicides die desiring something, if only revenge on the living.)

There is a surprising feature to Buddha's teaching that is seldom grasped by outsiders: it divides its deliverance from this dismal human condition into two steps. First, give up bad desires; second, give up good ones. Most Buddhists do not get past the first step of forsaking bad desires, hence elementary Buddhism is a force for good with its noble eightfold path: right views, right intentions, right speech, right conduct, right livelihood, right effort, right mindfulness, right meditation. It has foreign missionaries, as Americans know from seeing them on our streets; there is a Buddhist teacher in the religious departments of some American universities and a Buddhist chaplain in a state senate. "First-step" Buddhism has a Young Men's Buddhist Association and Buddhist Boy Scouts, and even a W.B.T.U. corresponding to the W.C.T.U. (Women's Christian Temperance Union) because Buddha like Muhammad forbade alcohol. These prohibitions led an early czar of Russia to favor Christianity when faced with a choice among the three religions.

The second step is the unique Buddhist surprise: after you make progress in doing good, then give up good because it is just as illusory as evil. Leave wife and children, abandon work, even in medicine or government, go out with begging bowl and saffron-yellow robe, the outcast's color symbolizing total detachment. Those who finally succeed in wanting nothing, neither evil nor good, may become unpersons forever, atoms of oxygen in an ocean of air. This fulfillment is sometimes called other-worldly although strictly it is no-worldly because it denies this world and the next; whereas Christianity claims both worlds, all this and

heaven too. The theological gulf makes the practical difference between East and West in science, government, and
everyday life. Buddhism withdraws its most devoted followers from family and work at age forty when they are
most needed by their children and country. It is one of
civilization's greatest brain drains. Hence many scholars
think Buddhism is not a reformation of Hinduism, but a
disastrous heresy, pushing non-attachment to fanatical
lengths as Hinduism rarely does.

It may occur to the reader that since by definition a religion is a relationship to God, neither Hinduism nor Buddhism is technically a religion because neither believes in
God. But this intellectual atheism is held only by the educated minority in both religions. Among the nonintellec-
tuals, Hinduism has a welter of gods and goddesses, temples, vigils, and devotional practices. And Buddha, the
atheist, is worshiped as a god by all but the most scholarly
Buddhists. These are further instances of the truth that
human beings are naturally religious in spite of exposure to
atheistic dogmas. Even when their world view teaches
them that there is no world view, the sense of the presence
of God haunts men. They may believe that the cosmos is an
illusion made intolerable by an endless transmigration of
souls, yet they still make an illogical place in it for a god or
gods. The transcendental comes in a plain brown envelope.
Ordinary believers see the sacrifices of their Hindu or Buddhist saints as intimations of immortality and divinity, no
matter how those saints deny it—another example of untidy theology reflecting untidy life.

My polemic against Buddhism reminds me of a pamphlet
on that religion slipped into my hand one day as I left an
Asian embassy. It was more anti-Christian than pro-
Buddhist and presented a sad distortion of Christianity. I
hope that what I have written about Buddhism is not as
prejudiced, but still, it must not be taken as the last word.
On the occasion when I was handed the tract with my hat

(the butler was probably an undercover missionary!), my host had outlined Buddhism to a group he had invited to meet a visiting Buddhist scholar. The ambassador, himself a devout Buddhist, explained that he believed in neither God nor prayer. Then while the saffron-robed monk at his side nodded approval, he went on to describe his great pleasure in America—going on Sunday to country churches in nearby Virginia and Maryland, singing hymns, and sensing the devoutness of the people. Or sometimes just sitting outside in his car watching them, white or black, Roman Catholic or Protestant, going into church and coming out with a different look on their faces. The ambassador is convinced he is looking at illusion but drives many miles every Sunday to see it. If he were true to his intellectual position, he would put on his robe and meditate on Nothingness, and not use gasoline and a chauffeur's time to be with people who seem to be helped by what he believes is not there at all.

Buddha by his own conduct attested to the drawing power of the goodness he claimed did not exist. His work was a sacrificial response to man's hunger for more than bread, and yet he thought that the mind is completely deceived by the illusion that there is even such a thing as bread, let alone anything after it. He taught that the only way to avoid being bothered by imaginary obligation is to abandon the whole concept of moral struggle—good and bad guys, cops and robbers, right and wrong. Everything is mental, as Alice was told in *Through the Looking-Glass*:

> "If the Red King left off dreaming about you . . . you'd be nowhere. Why, you're only a sort of thing in his dream!" said Tweedledee.
> "If that there King was to wake," added Tweedledum, "You'd go out—bang!—just like a candle."

Because Buddha believed in a totally subjective universe, he was tempted at first to practice his illumination alone and to let sleepwalking mankind go on in dreams without his awakening news. I don't see logically how he could have had any temptation to silence if there are no such things as morals or people. Disregarding consistency, Buddha decided at great personal sacrifice to spend laborious days sharing his insight with others. His kindness overcame his theology; "Do as I do, not as I say," was his legacy to the world. He was a great and holy man who spent his lifetime trying to quench the human thirst for information by which men live (or to tell them how they can escape altogether from living). In the end, he died of politeness, a touching inconsistency. Desperately ill, and warned by his physician not to eat meat, he was brought a roast of pork by a disciple who had killed a boar and cooked it for him. Since the disciple had gone to great pains, Buddha did not want to hurt his feelings by refusing. So he ate the meat and died in half an hour.

Islam

In much the same way as Buddhism is an offshoot of Hinduism, Islam (the religion of Muhammad) is an offshoot of the Bible, holding many things in common with the Bible's two religions, Christianity and Judaism. Like them, Islam believes that there is only one God and fiercely opposes any hint of plural gods. It holds that God (Allah) has created a solid world to be enjoyed and used as a school for the hereafter: "a vale for soul making." Existence is not an unreal dream from which religion offers an escape. Islam obeys the Ten Commandments and admires Jesus as a prophet in the long tradition of Isaiah, Jeremiah, on back to Moses. Judaism, Christianity, and Islam are all sons of Abraham; Jerusalem is a city that is sacred to three religions.

Islam claims that in the 600s Muhammad took the best in Judaism and Christianity and made a third and greater religion. It was a reform of the Bible that Muhammad accomplished by accepting the Mosaic Law, the Hebrew prophets, and Jesus's emphasis on love. From there, Muhammad went on to show specifically in the Koran (the Muslim Bible) how to carry out these precepts. He pointed out that Jesus himself had not had time to systematize his message, because he taught only one year, or at most three, while Muhammad taught for twenty-three years. This time factor is the first chasm between Islam and Christianity. Islam believes that no one can know what is right unless it is written out for him precisely, which is what Muhammad did with Jesus's beautiful but general insights. Christians instinctively reject this notion because they fear a lapse into the legalism that plagues all religions. They believe Muhammad misunderstood Christianity, where the primacy of spirit over law is a key principle. Put starkly, as Saint Augustine did, Christians love God and do as they please, flat against Islam's teaching that ethics can be practiced only if codified.

There is a second chasm between the two religions: followers of Muhammad dislike to be called Muhammadans; followers of Christ like to be called Christians. Muslims regard Muhammad as God's last and greatest prophet, not God Incarnate as Christians believe Christ to be. For this reason, they vehemently object to the designations *Muhammadan* for the believer and *Muhammadanism* for the faith, and prefer the names *Muslim* and *Islam*. To insist that Muhammad was only a messenger sounds modest and reasonable, a dogma that appeals to the undogmatic. Islam says that God did not come to earth Himself; Christianity says He did, which is a hard saying I'll come to at the end of this chapter.

Neither Muslim nor Christian prayers are mental escapes from a bad world. In both faiths the worshiper, unlike the Hindu and Buddhist, believes he is talking with a good Creator of a good universe. A Muslim prays five times a day: on arising, at noon, in the afternoon, after sunset, and at bedtime, not only in the mosque but anywhere, since all the world is God's. For this reason mosques have towers called minarets from which the muezzin (the crier) can urge the believer to pray wherever he happens to be.

How the Muslim prays is worth looking at in detail because it reinforces the value of ritualism. It begins with simple adoration, the kind of prayer that overbusy Westerners often do not appreciate. If there is water nearby when the Muslim hears the call to prayer, he washes his hands, face, and feet, spreads his prayer rug before him, and stands erect. Placing his hands at the side of his eyes to keep out distractions, he says, "Allahu akbar" (God is great). Still standing, he recites,

> Praise belongs to God, Lord of the Worlds,
> The Compassionate, the Merciful
> King of the day of judgment.

Then he bows low, hands on hips, and says, "I extol the perfection of my Lord, the Great." He returns to the upright position, again repeating, "God is great." Next he falls on his knees, putting forehead and hands on the ground (the fez or brimless hat comes from this), then rises to his knees and sits on his heels, and again touches his forehead to the ground.

His prayers are not primarily petitions for himself or others; they are worship and praise of the Almighty, the highest form of prayer, and the opposite of Hindu and Buddhist mental exercises. The ritual itself precludes embarrassment because it is conventional; everyone at the oil well or on the streets is doing it. A custom may end as an encounter with God. "Blue Domers" who claim they worship without ritual lack just such a routine as this Muslim one to force their attention on Him who made the dome blue.

Islam permits no statues or paintings of people or animals for fear of idolatry, which is forbidden by the Bible's

Second Commandment (the one against making images). The designs in its mosques are either geometric or derived from their calligraphy. Muslims have a particular aesthetic feeling for the spoken word, since in their early nomadic life in the desert, living in tents, they had to abandon books, musical instruments, and all permanent loveliness; only human speech remained to describe life's mystery and beauty. Worshipers are moved by the very cadences of the muezzin's recitation from the minaret: *La ilaha illa Allah*, "There is no God but Allah." Islam originally had few cities and is tuned to the outdoors. The Koran attracts nature lovers with its recollection of blazing desert and glorious hills, the Muslim counterpart of the Psalms of David, Saint Francis of Assisi's canticle "Praised be my Lord for our brother sun," Saint Patrick's Breastplate "I bind unto myself today . . . the whirling wind's tempestuous shocks," and Jesus's parable about the lilies of the field "I say unto you, That even Solomon in all his glory was not arrayed like one of these" (*Matthew* 6:28–29). Later, when Islam was established in the cities of Spain and North Africa, architecture and gardening became two of its glories, elements of which have been copied all over the world.

There is a striking asceticism in Islam. For the strict Muslim there's no alcohol or gambling, and one-fortieth of his entire possessions is to be given to charity every year. The bravery of Turkish soldiers and the incorruptibility of their policemen are proverbial. Islam's polygamy may be excused as Muhammad's alternative to the sexual promiscuity of his people in the seventh century. As time went on, polygamy was perpetuated by economic factors and the killing off of males in tribal warfare. Now polygamy is disappearing because of the educational emancipation of women in advanced countries. In old-fashioned Islamic lands, however, women are still sequestered and go out covered by veils. Slavery is still permitted in parts of Islam a hundred years after Christendom abolished it, but a hundred years is not much to boast about, and even now some Christian nations in Africa are suspect.

Islamic countries are backward industrially, because of the Koran's archaic laws governing interest, property, and inheritance. Religious law is still more important than civil law; political structures vary from feudal to totalitarian with little social mobility between classes. Muslims are a prey to tyranny because they have never yet had freedom; having always lived under religious autocracy, they can accept new political dictators from right or left.

The words *Islam* and *Muslim* are derived from the Arabic *salaam*, the peace that comes from submission to Allah's pattern of life, believed to be unalterable. Instead of expecting fresh instruction from God's living Spirit, Muslims have only their ancient code book, the Koran. This is the answer to the disparity between Jesus's few years and Muhammad's twenty-three years of teaching. Said colloquially, Christians believe that the Holy Spirit took up where Jesus left off. "It is expedient for you that I go away; for if I go not away, the Comforter will not come unto you; but if I depart, I will send him unto you" (*John* 16:7).

On the intellectual side, Islam has never come to terms with modern knowledge; its science is backward, although it was once in the vanguard. (Arabic numerals are still in use.) In World War II, African Bedouins destroyed United States Air Force weather stations because they believed forecasting the wind was prying into Allah's secrets. (He alone decides what the weather will be, hence predicting it is irreligious.) It is considered equally blasphemous to suppose that trachoma comes from dirty flies, because Allah predetermines which children will be blind. The Koran has little of the Bible's appeal to logic; it triumphed less by persuasion than by the sword. In many African nations today this choice between the Koran and death is the hidden cause of bloodshed more than the tribalism and colonialism reported in the news. Islam is ordinarily state-supported, and it only minimally tolerates other faiths.

It might be fair to say that the "silken curtain," which Islam stretched across North Africa from the seventh century until the seventeenth, cut off that whole continent from the Christian and classical thought of the Mediterranean basin and explains why Africa never developed as Europe did. The people of Africa today are no more backward than our remote ancestors were when they painted themselves blue and roamed the forests of Northern Europe. But our ancestors were exposed to centuries of Christian missions and Greco-Roman civilization. Africa is now trying to absorb in a few decades what Europe learned in a thousand years.

Islam's influence at first was good; it gloriously transformed the polytheism and moral degradation of North Africa. Muhammad was a second Moses who freed his people from superstition and established an empire that stretched from Turkey to Spain and, after his death, grew larger than Alexander's or Caesar's. Architecture, medicine, and mathematics flourished; the Greek classics were preserved by Islam when Europe banished them. What happened to bring on the present chaos?

One explanation is that Islam is a step forward for primitive societies but has little to offer advanced ones. Its two chief theological errors, that God did not come to earth (no Son of God) and that His continuing direction is not available (no Holy Spirit) add up to a denial of the Trinity, if you don't mind the dogmatic digression. Religious scholars maintain that Islam is a Bible heresy as Buddhism is a Hindu heresy, and like all heresies, they lead to bad social results beginning with the poor and eventually reaching everyone. Buddhism is partly to blame for the brain drain of Asia, Islam for the backwardness of Africa and the Middle East. A religion's later results are as important as its initial impact. Does the faith renew itself? Can a lost radiance be recovered? Religions are judged by their social results, and for this reason they are sometimes classified in college catalogues under sociology. The working out of the faith in life is the final test. "Ye shall know them by their fruits. Do men gather grapes of thorns, or figs of thistles?" (*Matthew* 7:16).

Failure of Nerve

To ask what religion does is like asking what color fruit is. Different religions do different things; the question must be asked about a particular religion. We have looked at three —Hinduism, Buddhism, and Islam—and named their most glaring differences from Christianity. Comparing religions is not that simple in actual practice. They are usually not presented to people in neat packages of Hinduism, Buddhism, Islam, and Christianity. Often they come as a conglomerate of contradictions from various faiths. Even the package labeled Christianity has not passed any food-and-drug inspection. Almost everyone has had a Christian Science uncle (who was truly cured of something) or a Mormon scoutmaster or a Pentecostal roommate at school. My own son had so many varieties of enthusiastic Christians in a large suite of college roommates that he had to study in the college library and after hours in the bathroom.

Here eclecticism enters. Gilbert Murray describes the dangerous consequences in his paragraph that ends with the often-quoted phrase, "failure of nerve."

It is a rise of asceticism, of mysticism, in a sense, of pessimism; a loss of self-confidence, of hope in this life and of faith in normal human effort; a despair of patient inquiry, a cry for infallible revelation; an indifference to the welfare of the state, a conversion of the soul to God. It is an atmosphere in which the aim of the good man is not so much to live justly, to help the society to which he belongs and enjoy the esteem of his fellow creatures; but rather, by means of a burning faith, by contempt of the world and its standards, by ecstasy, suffering, and martyrdom, to be granted pardon for his unspeakable unworthiness, his immeasurable sins. There is an intensifying of certain spiritual emotions; an increase of sensitiveness, a failure of nerve.

Such phenomena annoy the agnostic, and rightly. Why, he fumes, should a rise of mysticism lead to pessimism? Shouldn't religion be cheerful about elementary duties? Why should ecstasy smother ordinary obligations? The questioner's indignation reveals that he has grown up with a Christian background, because the Bible condemns almost everything in Professor Murray's catalogue. He was describing the classical world before Christ, when the Greco-Roman failure of nerve came from mixing religions without discrimination. The difficulty was not too much religion but too many odd ingredients. The ancient world held to an unthinking syncretism made possible by travel on the safe roads of the Pax Romana. The same kind of practice is made possible by the jet travel of the twentieth century. Such minglings of religions force two questions: First, is there anything special about Christianity? The answer is not always clear to Christians, and thinking it out is clouded by their fear of appearing sectarian, so it seems more broadminded to throw together a potpourri of faiths. Second, a more drastic question is, if bad results can come from religion, why not do away with it altogether? The answer is that religion cannot be abolished, it can only be educated. Religion can bless or curse mankind with endless gradations, depending on how God is perceived and on what His followers believe He wants them to do.

A lady tells every clergyman she meets about the Arab taxi driver who took her to see the pyramids. He complained of a toothache, and she offered him a swig of the brandy she carried as a seasoned traveler. He declined, saying, "No, Madam, I have never tasted alcohol." (He was, of course, a devout Muslim.) After another half-hour of his groans, she said, "Why don't you just hold some of the brandy in your mouth without swallowing? Perhaps the alcohol will relieve the pain." But he continued steadfast in his refusal. The climax of her story is, "After that taxi ride, I shall never give another cent to Christian missions!"

President Roosevelt, making conversation with his Navy chaplain on the way to Hawaii during the war, said, "Padre, I tell my mother she's a murderer!" Politely surprised, the chaplain asked, "How is that, sir?," and the President got off the one about the missionaries to Hawaii putting the naked natives into Mother Hubbard dresses, which gave them pneumonia, and so they died, hence everyone who contributes to missions is a murderer.

Such theological gamesmanship is not as serious as the bewilderment of people who wonder why they are being forced to choose between religions. They long for the old days when they suppose the whole world agreed about God and right and wrong. Well, everyone did agree, but only with those in his own small circle, and there were no overlapping circles to make him aware of dissent. One's neighborhood was the whole world. Now all believers are confronted with a wide variety of faiths. They meet many different religions in the Services, or in changing jobs, or at vacation resorts. Few grow up in a neighborhood where all are Baptist or Roman Catholic or Muslim. Christians are holding forbidden services behind closed doors in Arab nations; Protestants are entering the Latin countries of Europe and South America; and Roman Catholics are beginning to make headway in the deep South.

The old-fashioned course in comparative religion seldom compared differing religions. It emphasized their resemblances in spite of their variety but never evaluated their results; consequently there appeared to be no basis for choosing between them. The phrase "comparative religion" (singular) implied to generations of students that religion is all one thing. (Comparative shopping does just the opposite in competitive business studies.) Perhaps the theological study should be named "comparing religions" (plural) to emphasize the differences in their consequences. A recent college graduate told me about a beautiful Pakistani girl he had fallen in love with at the United Nations. "She's a Muslim, but I told her, you know, that all religions are alike—Catholicism, Hinduism, and Presbyterianism—you know, what I learned in Comparative Religion at school." My astonishment showed so plainly that he stopped, and I told him that such confusion of mind could only result in mixed-up matrimony.

The compelling reason for studying other religions is to understand and practice our own. Non-Christian faiths should shake up our Christianity and make it more an authentic bearer of the Divine Message. It is from others that we learn how great is the gulf between true Christianity and how we practice it. For the believer, the searching questions are always comparative: Am I a mystic who is weak on work? Am I a worker who prays too little? Does the child's prayer convict me? ("Dear God, please make the bad people good and the good people nice.") Have I what Phillips Brooks called "the gently complaining voice of the liberal"? Do I avoid *agape*, as it appears in the guise of creamed chicken at church socials? Such personal questions are gathered up in the *Book of Common Prayer*: "Judge therefore yourselves, brethren, that ye be not judged of the Lord; repent you truly for your sins past; amend your lives, and be in perfect charity with all men."

Church congregations as well as individuals profit by self-assessment. The difference between congregations is not that one has a contemporary building and the other a gothic, that one's liturgy is experimental and another's traditional. The important distinctions are deeper. Parishes are exposed to their minister's current enthusiasms, cerebral, moralistic, aesthetic, or hyperactivist, and come out for a time half-baked. "Ephraim is a cake not turned" (*Hosea* 7:8). Hence the diversified churches need one another, as diversified believers need one another. They gradually learn to value each other's partialities, and this is the bright side of idiosyncrasies. Believers come to see that it is good that one likes to teach, another to evangelize, still another to fight for social justice. Christians are meant to differ in nonessentials; everyone is not supposed to be like every other one: "Are all apostles? are all prophets? are all teachers? are all workers of miracles? have all the gifts of healing? do all speak with tongues? do all interpret?" asks Paul in *1 Corinthians* 12:29–30, which leads into his hymn to love in Chapter 13. Earlier he writes: "For the body is not one member, but many. . . . And the eye cannot say unto the hand, I have no need of thee: nor again the head to the feet, I have no need of you. . . . That there should be no schism in the body; but that the members should have the same care one for another. . . . Now ye are the body of Christ, and members in particular" (*1 Corinthians* 12:14, 21, 25, 27).

This love for brethren who have different talents is especially important when presuming to judge other faiths. A Christian does not beard a Hindu with, "Where do you get this nonmaterial stuff?", although he may ask about polygamy if a Muslim wants to marry his daughter. The wise missionary never attacks native religions in spite of the single-mindedness for Christ that sent him into voluntary exile. "Is he to believe that the loving God and merciful Redeemer has been so fanciful, if not so cruel, as to leave the nonbeliever in total darkness and error?" asks a Catholic missionary in India, echoing Peter long ago at Caesarea:

"Of a truth I perceive that God is no respecter of persons: But in every nation he that feareth him, and worketh righteousness, is accepted with him" (*Acts* 10: 34–35).

Above all, to discriminate among religions is not to think that any Christian is better than any Hindu, but that faith in Christ is better than faith in Krishna because it will lead him deeper into a knowledge of God and man. In fact, so much deeper that Christians claim Christianity is not one of the religions of the world, it *is* religion. For this reason, a person will rarely say that he is a good Christian but rather that he is a good churchman, or a good Catholic, or a good Baptist, or that he goes to church regularly. It sounds less pretentious than claiming to be a good Christian and means he humbly belongs to a learning circle, as the Negro spiritual sings, "Lord, I want to be a Christian in my heart." No one dares pray, "Lord, revive thy Church," who does not hastily add, "beginning with me."

Christian Materialism

The greatest idiosyncrasy of Christianity is its involvement with the material world, flat against the popular idea that religion should be "spiritual." Hindus and Buddhists are quick to bring up this Christian quality whenever they are faulted for their noninvolvement with practical matters. Even the Muslims, who theoretically side with the Christians on materialism, criticize them for being too materialistic and boast of their own asceticism. It crosses the sociologist's mind, however, that Muslims are forced to live simply perhaps because the few rich keep the good things away from the many poor. And the Muslim teaching about heaven is far from ascetic but thoroughly sensuous. In theory, however, Christians and Muslims agree theologically that this is a solid earth, made to be enjoyed. "The greatest poverty," wrote the poet Wallace Stevens, "is not to live in a physical world."

The importance of the physical to Christians is another conclusion derived from their Bible. An adverb in the first chapter gives a lilt to all subsequent history. "God saw every thing that he had made, and, behold, it was *very* good" (*Genesis* 1:31) (italics added). Anyone who knows the Bible at least from A to B would be familiar with prosperity, the subject of the first book, and with liberty, the subject of the second. *Genesis* is a Robinson Crusoe story; *Exodus*, a Fourth of July oration. These two books alone make the Bible the Magna Carta of the poor and enslaved. Prosperity and liberty were promised in the 1917 Bolshevik revolution as "Bread, Land, and Peace." Bread and land were prosperity, peace was liberty; no one wanted to continue the old martial-law "peace" of czarism. Yet czarist peace is what the Soviet continued, and as for plenteousness, a democratic revolution would have given the proletariat much more.

In 1940, Puerto Rico launched Operation Bootstrap on a platform of bread, land, and freedom, the same Bible hopes. In 1956, the short revolt in Poland had a slogan, "Bread and Freedom," *Genesis* and *Exodus* again. The sudden sound of these first promises of the Bible was intoxicating after years of false slogans, and resulted in the Hungarian revolt, also ended by Russian tanks. In 1970, Poland took to the streets again for more consumer goods in the stores, a modern equivalent of the herds and flocks of *Genesis*. Men die for liberty in a world of meat and potatoes. "The spiritual is everywhere dependent on the material. This is depressingly and magnificently obvious. To think we must eat" (Teilhard de Chardin).

Speculation about why this is true returns to the fact that the only universe we know is both matter and spirit. It is not news; the question is, does it also go the other way?

Can ideas influence bodily functions? Certainly they influence the flow of blood to the brain; if not, what is fainting? "The joints of his loins were loosed" (*Daniel* 5:6) means the king was so frightened he soiled his clothing. Fear supplies adrenaline to make us run faster, and worry brings ulcers to slow us down; thus in many elementary ways, thoughts control matter. Possibly there is rudimentary awareness on every level of life—daisies may enjoy themselves, and poison ivy be ashamed; perhaps the alfalfa doesn't grow because the farmer doesn't give it enough love. Certainly when we come to animals, mind has some control over matter, and with man there is evidence of large control.

Michael Faraday, the nineteenth-century scientist who made possible Thomas Edison's twentieth-century discoveries, presented the question thus:

> Six or seven years ago whilst standing at the door of a gentleman's house and waiting until my knock should be answered, I thrust my head through some iron railing that separated the doorway from another and then I began to consider on which side of the rail I was. In my mind I affirmed that the side possessing my head was my station for there was my perception, my senses. I had just sufficient time to ascertain this when the door opened and my nose began bleeding by the contact of the rail and such matter as that quickly put flight to my rude metaphysics. Simple as is this instance, it did more in illustrating this case to me than all the arguments I have heard since on the subject.

By such simple instances, everyone sees the material as part of the spiritual and the spiritual as part of the material. "In the kingdom of God men are created with flesh, reconciled through flesh, and glorified as flesh. To hide from the flesh for the sake of the spirit is to miss the Christian life" (Arthur McGill).

Christian dogma says that the material things of life are for everyone; it does not despise them nor argue that deprivation is a higher style of life. It believes every person should live well but simply; Americans with a chicken in every pot, Hottentots with a quart of milk, the Soviet with bread, land, and peace; and Poles, Hungarians, and other satellites with such consumer goods as they can manage between tank visits. Dame Edith Evans after seventy years on the British stage was asked how she was able to keep her lovely complexion and carry on brilliantly for so long. Her formula was, "Lots of soap and water; and I believe in God." Mentioning soap before God does not bother theologians; the greatly admired Salvation Army's priority in saving souls is scrubology before theology; its sequence of events for the down-and-out is soup, soap, and salvation.

William Temple wrote:

> One ground for the hope of Christianity that it may make good its claim to be the true faith lies in the fact that it is the most avowedly materialistic of all the great religions. It affords an expectation that it may be able to control the material, precisely because it does not ignore it or deny it, but roundly asserts alike the reality of matter and its subordination. Its own most central saying is: "The Word was made flesh," where the last term was, no doubt, chosen because of its specially materialistic associations.

Temple's words must be looked at carefully; in his good writing an adverb is rare. "*Avowedly* materialistic," he writes, possibly because Christians can be misled by avowedly spiritualistic religions. Robert Frost reminds us, in "Kitty Hawk":

> Westerners inherit
> A design for living
> Deeper into matter—
> Not without due patter
> Of a great misgiving.

The due patter of a great misgiving is the unwarranted assumption that the spiritual can ignore the material. The Bible denies this; many passages reinforce the primary emphasis in *Genesis* on wealth and riches. From the Psalms: "O pray for the peace of Jerusalem; they shall prosper that love thee. Peace be within thy walls, and plenteousness within thy palaces. For my brethren and companions' sakes, I will wish thee prosperity" (122:6–8). From the Gospel: "There is no man that hath left house, or brethren, or sisters, or father, or mother, or wife, or children, or lands, for my sake, and the gospel's, But he shall receive an hundredfold now in this time, houses, and brethren, and sisters, and mothers, and children, and lands, with persecutions; and in the world to come eternal life" (*Mark* 10:29–30).

Frost says:

> . . . God's own descent
> Into flesh was meant
> As a demonstration
> That the supreme merit
> Lay in risking spirit
> In substantiation.

The Incarnation

Substantiation is another word for "incarnation," the crux of Christianity. It is the belief that God came to this physical earth, risking spirit in substantiation. Christianity is Christ; Christmas, or Christ's mass, is the celebration of his birth. The whole Western world, playboy and puritan alike,

sing about it in churches, at Rotary lunches, at office parties, in glee clubs, and around the piano at home:

> O come, all ye faithful,
> Joyful and triumphant,
> O come ye, O come ye to Bethlehem;
> Come and behold him,
> Born the King of angels;
> O come, let us adore him, Christ the Lord.

The singers stumble over the second stanza where the idea
is made painfully explicit:

> God of God,
> Light of Light,
> Lo! he abhors not the Virgin's womb;
> Very God,
> Begotten, not created;
> O come, let us adore him, Christ the Lord.

It is hard to fit these words to the music, let alone to clear
thinking. "Very God, begotten, not created" is an insight
that came first to the Jews, was written down in Greek, and
was translated into Latin, and eventually into every language. It says that God became man, that He was enclosed
in material flesh. This is what Christians call the Incarnation, and it has been said that no one has the right to believe it who has not at first thought it incredible. Most
carolers do not understand it and are glad to get to the
third stanza:

> Yea, Lord, we greet thee,
> Born this happy morning;
> Jesus, to thee be glory given;
> Word of the Father,
> Now in flesh appearing;
> O come, let us adore him, Christ the Lord.

But this stanza is equally incredible. How can a word appear in flesh? How can it be said that Christian teaching is simple when its intellectual basis is so complex? It is ironic that the simplicity/complexity nettle has to be grasped at Christmas when everything is supposed to become more childlike.

The carols try for two truths that seem contradictory. First, Jesus Christ is the Son of God. He is not a prophet, or a principle of concretion, or a rallying point for idealism; He is God Himself come into the world. Second, He was human. He suffered, He was tempted, hungry and thirsty, sad and happy, certain and uncertain, as we are. He appeared in the world as we all do, born of a woman, not like the ancient god who came to earth in the form of a bull or a shower of gold, or like Athena springing from Zeus's forehead, and in contrast to Father Divine, who claimed he was never born but was "combusted" on the sidewalks of New York City. "Lo, he abhors not the Virgin's womb" or "Thou didst humble thyself to be born of a Virgin" says that Jesus was born like any other human being even though that fact demeaned him in the eyes of the Greco-Roman world. How a man can be God on earth will be discussed and rephrased by scholars for each new generation, but in the meantime the double truth is sung: Jesus is God, Jesus is man.

Thinking it out can begin with negatives. If Jesus is *not* divine, then what he did was *not* God's own venture. Instead of risking spirit in substantiation, God sent an agent, not His only begotten son, not part of His Very Being. The agonizing human question has always been, does God help or does He watch the human struggle without caring? The Greeks believed the gods stay out of earthly concerns; classical sculpture showed them with passionless faces even in battle. When Prometheus, suffering on the rock, cries, "Alas!," Hermes coolly reminds him, "Zeus does not know the meaning of the word." Indifference was a heavenly trait to the Greek; to be disengaged was the mark of divinity. The Stoic who called Jesus vulgar gave two examples—his weeping and his turning the other cheek—both showing an involvement that to the Stoic was contemptible. Pythagoras illustrated heaven's detachment by describing three kinds of people at the Olympic games: the athlete struggling for victory, the vendor trying to sell the ancient equivalent of popcorn, and the aloof spectator in the stadium. Pythagoras said it was only the spectator who was godlike because concern about winning or selling betrays human weakness. Christianity holds that God is concerned; it points to the cross and says God loves like that.

Christ's divinity, or his deity (words that are interchangeable in common speech), may be partly grasped by imagining a workman who falls off a bridge and is rescued from drowning. He will want to know who pulled him out; was it one of his fellow laborers, or was it the boss himself? So men ask, was Jesus a fellow human being or God Incarnate? To multiply adjectives and make Jesus the best, best, best man who ever lived is still never the same as saying that he is God's only begotten son. A superstar is an extraordinarily able star, but Jesus is more. He is God. This distinction is important because it is saying something about God, not about Jesus; it actually says God is like Jesus when it claims Jesus is like God. The unknown (God) is explained by the known (Jesus). To a country boy you say a helicopter looks like a threshing machine; to a city boy you say a threshing machine looks like a helicopter. There are many metaphors, all making the essential point that "God was in Christ, reconciling the world unto himself" (*2 Corinthians* 5:19).

When in turn we try to think out Jesus's humanity, this line of thought can also begin with negatives. If he is *not* human, he *cannot* be our example because he did *not* live under our conditions. He is like the Arabian Nights caliph who went out to visit the poor in their hovels but came home every night to a warm bath and a clean bed. Any description of Jesus that in the slightest way denies his humanness is wrong; his deity does not make him magically superior to his contemporaries, like Superman in the comic strips or the Connecticut Yankee at King Arthur's Court. What scholars call the "birth narratives" (the Roman census, the stable, the flight into Egypt) are important as establishing the fact of a real baby and a real family's struggle to survive. Increasing "in wisdom and stature, and in favour with God and man" (*Luke* 2:52) describes a maturing boy. "Is not this the carpenter?" (*Mark* 6:3) brings the answer, yes, he is a carpenter, not a disguised emissary using a hammer and saw as a cover. His life is an incarnation, not a masquerade.

A masquerade life is portrayed in what are sometimes titled *The Forbidden Books of the Bible*. Republished every few years, they are advertised as revealing information about Jesus that the Church suppressed. Actually, the Church did not suppress these books but discarded them because their legends included absurd stories that were supposed to prove Jesus's divinity. One such story described a day in his childhood when he was making mud images of birds. Because it was the Sabbath, a rabbi rebuked him, whereupon the child said a magic word and the statues turned into live birds and flew away. Another instance has Jesus, as a young carpenter, carrying a beam and bumping into a fellow worker who thereupon cursed him. A glance from Jesus struck the man dead. Such tales, from ludicrous to monstrous, were not included when the Bible was put together, because they deny Jesus's humanity.

Even the miracles are not proof of his divinity as commonly supposed but of his magnificent humanity. He expressly denied that wonders were evidence of divinity, and he told his disciples that through God they could do the miracles he did and even greater ones (see *The Acts of the Apostles*). Christians still do astonishing things. A reformed drunkard remarked that he does not know whether Christ turned water into wine at Cana of Galilee, but at his house Christ turned beer into furniture. The fact that Christ passed on to other men his powers of healing shows that his miracles constituted no breach of the cosmic process and that he wished us to understand this.

However difficult to hold in the mind the apparent contradiction that Jesus is both God and man, people enjoy singing this truth from earliest childhood in the carols. Many other happy Christmas customs crowd memory, like the pageant of the Wise Men. Tradition says one of them was a Negro, and a black boy was always one of the Magi, or a white child blacked up to take the part. The ideal that all races are one in Christ was spread through pageantry long before racial tolerance had made much progress and may have had an early influence on it.

No one ever forgets the excitement of Christmas morning in childhood and the first sight of the decorated tree with the presents underneath. Later when he helped his parents stuff the stockings to surprise the younger children, and still later when he trimmed the tree for his own children, the happiness increased. Every family has traditions that came flooding back. In some homes a child memorizes the Bible account of the Nativity and another recites " 'Twas the Night Before Christmas." I was taken every Christmas time to the planetarium in New York and shown a star crossing from the East to Bethlehem, too young to wonder how it could be made to travel at camel's pace or whether the star's positions had been turned back to A.D. zero or a more accurate date for Jesus's birth. Afterward we would go next door to the Museum of Natural History, where a whale skeleton hung overhead. I did wonder whether Jonah could slide down that throat, yet my faith was never upset by the science-religion bind that bothered teenagers before World War I. I don't know why; perhaps it was because my early education was scientific, we always went to church, and I assumed these activities were somehow compatible. Perhaps it was because I grew up in a Jewish neighborhood and learned poetry in the theater. In Sunday school, I first heard what a simile was: "The mountains skipped like rams, and the little hills like young sheep" (*Psalm* 114:4). "Children," our minister told us, "mountains don't skip, but if you're happy they seem to." Later I tried to explain poetry to my own children while I struggled to make an electric Christmas star travel up the aisle of the church and cautioned small shepherds to keep their crooks out of each other's eyes.

As we recall our happy memories of Christmas, we keep in mind that Hindus, Buddhists, and Muslims also have joyous holy days and home customs, their haunting melodies and lights, and the love of parents and children. Childhood impressions are not the material for thinking out our faith. What we think in maturity is the basis for forming our convictions.

For Christians the happy memories come especially with the carols, and however complex the ideas, the words have to be plain. Dean Swift read his stuff to the stable boys, and Franklin Roosevelt tried out his fireside chats on the man who pushed his wheelchair. The Church does this with its teaching and tries in every age to restate an intellectual faith in the simplest possible words. The basic truths never alter, even though fashions come and go in theology as they do in every branch of learning and athletics (good professional football players last only ten years). Cocktail-party philosophers ask, "Whatever became of The-Medium-is-the-Message Marshall McLuhan?," as in an earlier day they tried to recall the first name of Dr. Coué ("Every day, in every way, I'm getting better and better"). Just so, good theologians come and go about every ten years. But the truth does not change, although it is expressed in changing words. And the singing goes on steadily:

O little town of Bethlehem
How still we see thee lie!
Above thy deep and dreamless sleep
The silent stars go by;
Yet in thy dark streets shineth
The everlasting Light;
The hopes and fears of all the years
Are met in thee tonight.

How silently, how silently,
The wondrous gift is given!
So God imparts to human hearts
The blessings of his heaven.
No ear may hear his coming,
But in this world of sin,
Where meek souls will receive him, still
The dear Christ enters in.

Six

EVANGELISM

Knowing How to Keep Christmas Well

The early Church celebrated Christ's coming into the world on Epiphany, January 6, long before it set aside Christmas Day, December 25. *Epiphany* is Greek for "showing forth," and the early Christians were saying that a grown man appeared in the world with saving power, not that a helpless baby was born in a stable. The chief symbol of Christianity has always been Jesus on the cross, not the Babe in the manger with the animals, shepherds, and wise men.

This showing forth of Christ is called evangelism, a word loved by some and scorned by others all through the ages. In 1976, when the newly appointed Archbishop of Canterbury spoke in Washington Cathedral, he said he was an evangelist. He was humorously deprecating himself, but at the same time Archbishop Coggan was seriously saying that he hoped he was leading the Anglican Communion to do its part with all Christian churches in proclaiming Christ. He used the name that Bunyan's Pilgrim said belonged to a "very great and honorable person; his name as I remember is Evangelist." Yet even Bunyan hints at misgivings about the name Evangelist by his tentative "as I remember."

Evangelism arouses dislike by what I referred to in the passage on social grace as the graceless behavior of some evangelists: adolescents with new-found faith trying to convert their saintly elders, a religious form of teaching grandmother to suck eggs; fanatics disfiguring the landscape with signs, "Prepare to meet thy God." Jesus had scathing words about those who "compass sea and land to make one proselyte, and when he is made, ye make him twofold more the child of hell than yourselves" (*Matthew* 23:15). The denigration of evangelism is so widespread that to describe a religion as nonmissionary often seems to commend it. Yet to knowledgeable Christians, mission is the compelling word. I went to a seminary whose graduates were classified either as missionaries or as second-class clergymen, and I belonged, regretfully, to the latter group. The students were taught that outreach is a controlling truth; that the very first thing to do if you are sent to a broken-down parish is to take up a collection for overseas missions. Martin Luther said that he who has found Christ must become a Christ to other people. Pontifex Maximus, Chief Bridge Maker, was the religious title of the pagan Roman emperors, later adopted by the popes. No matter who is *maximus*, every Christian is a *pontifex*, a bridge maker.

Evangelism is the whole point of Dickens's beloved *Christmas Carol*. When Scrooge's nephew wishes him a merry Christmas, the old miser says, "Bah! Humbug!" and angrily refuses to give to the charity committee who call on him. Actually he was not objecting to Christmas but to Epiphany. Even Scrooge could not object to the Holy Child; what he shrank from was involvement with other people. Yet this reaching out of Epiphany is the real spirit of the celebration for those who know how to keep Christmas well, as Scrooge was to learn from his three ghostly visitors.

Epiphany

The Incarnation (God going into the world) is put back-
wards by the well-loved stories of shepherds coming to
Christ's cradle and wise men journeying to find him. They
imply that the lowest and highest came to him instead of
his going to them. This image is perpetuated in hymns like
"We Three Kings of Orient Are," the Epiphany star in
churches, and the pictures and stained glass of the centuries, all of which unwittingly proclaim that everyone
seeks Christ, whereas the prior truth is that Christ seeks
everyone. "We love him, because he first loved us" (*1 John*
4:19). The Incarnation is God coming to man, "risking
spirit in substantiation."

If this seems like hairsplitting, consider what everyone
knows: the most joyous part about the holy season is planning presents and parties for others, not receiving gifts and
being entertained ourselves; it is Epiphany that is merry,
not Christmas. Older people sometimes say sadly that they
haven't enjoyed Christmas since they were children opening packages. They forget that they had an even greater
pleasure when giving packages to their children, surprising
friends with gifts and messages, and writing checks to char-
ities. These were the things Scrooge fiercely avoided until
he was converted by the three spirits who came to haunt
him. A person's age has nothing to do with Christmas, because giving happiness (often conspiratorial) need never
end. Christmas is Epiphany.

Samuel Eliot Morison used Epiphany in the broadest
sense in his *European Discovery of America:*

> Let us not forget that this century was also an Epi-
> phany in the religious sense; the main conception and
> aim of Columbus, to carry the Word of God and
> knowledge of His Son to the far corners of the globe,

became a fact: Christ had been made manifest to a new race of Gentiles. By 1615 the Christian Mass was being celebrated in hundreds of churches from the St. Lawrence through the Antilles to the River Plate, and along the west coast from Valdivia to Lower California. To the people of this New World, pagans expecting short and brutish lives, void of hope for any future, had come the Christian vision of a merciful God and a glorious Heaven. And from the decks of ships traversing the two great oceans and exploring the distant verges of the earth, prayers arose like clouds of incense to the Holy Trinity and to Mary, Queen of the Sea.

The Christmas carol "O Little Town of Bethlehem," has an Epiphany stanza (alas, often omitted):

> Where children pure and happy
>   Pray to the blessed Child,
> Where misery cries out to thee,
>   Son of the mother mild;
> Where charity stands watching
>   And faith holds wide the door,
> The dark night wakes, the glory breaks,
>   And Christmas comes once more.

Today Epiphany attracts altruists who don't know the translation of the Greek, and most of them would be astonished to hear their work called evangelism. What else, as already suggested, is foreign aid and domestic social service? To get appropriations voted, foreign aid may be labeled self-defense, and social service may be labeled "cooling the cities," but both are mixed with large generosity. They are the counterpart of the Church's overseas and domestic mission except for size; government help is in billions, and mission is the women's sewing circle in the basement of the village church. Both enterprises suffer from the Ugly American stereotype, wasted money, and sudden destruction of long-nurtured projects. Foreign Service officers on furlough, who wonder how they can introduce a better life in the places where they are posted, begin to sound like the missionaries they sometimes scorn. They are obeying the old command without knowing it.

> Take up the White Man's burden—
>   Send forth the best ye breed—
> Go bind your sons to exile
>   To serve your captives' need;
> To wait in heavy harness
>   On fluttered folk and wild—
> Your new-caught, sullen peoples,
>   Half devil and half child.

Kipling's first line has gone out of fashion. His poem "The White Man's Burden, 1899" was addressed to isolationism when Americans started the Philippines on their fifty-year road to independence. After a century, it might be rewritten as "The Strong Man's Burden, 1999":

> Take up the strong man's burden—
>   The savage wars of peace—
> Fill full the mouth of Famine
>   And bid the sickness cease;
> Take up the strong man's burden—
>   Ye dare not stoop to less—
> Nor call too loud on Freedom
>   To cloak your weariness.
>
> Take up the strong man's burden—
>   And reap his old reward:
> The blame of those ye better,
>   The hate of those ye guard—

The cry of hosts ye humour
(Ah, slowly!) toward the light!
"Why brought ye us from bondage,
Our loved Egyptian night?"

The poem could also be recycled as "The Epiphany Burden, *Any Year*." In 1859, Abraham Lincoln commented on some 1776 words that might have been said over and over in our Bicentennial Year, 1976:

> These . . . representatives in old Independence Hall said to the whole world of men: "We hold these truths to be self-evident: that all men are created equal; that they are entitled to life, liberty and the pursuit of happiness." . . . This was their lofty, and wise, and noble understanding of the justice of the Creator to His creatures. Yes, gentlemen, to all His creatures, to the whole great family of man. . . . They grasped not only the whole race of man then living, but they reached forward and seized upon the farthest posterity.

He hoped, he said afterward, that he himself might become an instrument in the hands of the Almighty "and of this, His almost chosen people, for perpetuating the object of that great struggle." In 1973 Lincoln's words were echoed by Henry Kissinger when he was sworn in as Secretary of State. "America has never been true to itself unless it meant something beyond itself. As we work for a world at peace with justice, compassion and humanity, we know that America, in fulfilling man's deepest aspirations, fulfills what is best within it."

In 1959, when Hawaii became the fiftieth American state, it was a happy conjunction of evangelism, the Declaration of Independence, Epiphany, colonialism, Genesis prosperity, and Exodus liberty. It is true that in the 1830s mistakes were made by the first missionaries, like putting

the natives into heavy clothing, which was unhealthful in
that country. But the missionaries wore the same clothing
and many of them died. Their physiology was wrong, not
their theology; wool was the culprit, not prudery. For centuries, the naked poor had been scratched by branches and
bitten by insects until the missionaries introduced the
manufacture of cloth and finally discovered the right
weight for that climate. The natives were glad to get any
clothing and didn't have to be coerced into wearing it.

Another scoff about Hawaii is that at the beginning the
missionaries had the Bible and the natives had the land, but
in the end the natives had the Bible and the missionaries
had the land. Actually only a small aristocracy ever held
land in feudal Hawaii, and the missionaries did not pass it
from Queen to Church but from Queen to people. Land is
well distributed today; the notion that five missionary families rule the islands is tourist cocktail conversation. The
children of the early missionaries were sent home to college
in America, and when they returned to Hawaii bringing
their friends, they developed agriculture, education, trade,
and government. The missionaries themselves never prof-
ited from these unintended by-products of missions, but
they did start Hawaii on the long road that resulted in
statehood. This is not to say that statehood is the kingdom
of heaven; only that it was an Epiphany in the Pacific, as
Columbus's voyage was an Epiphany in the Atlantic.

Church Statistics

Since Hawaii, how has Epiphany been going? What has
Christian mission been doing? How well have Christians
been keeping Christmas? These are variations of the same
question and are often answered by statistics, which have
given such extraordinary results in science. "A recent survey shows" is an authoritative preamble. One statistic,

"Episcopalians are denser in the colleges," aroused a church to the importance of its ministry in higher education. It was a whimsical way of saying that the college population had a greater proportion of Episcopalians than the general population—that is, the percentage in Cornell was higher than in Philadelphia—although the most active pastors and parishes were in the cities rather than in the college towns. The figure startled parents who had children away at college, and as a consequence more clergy and stronger churches have been put into university centers over the past thirty-five years. A corresponding need, to provide more able chaplains for the armed services, has not yet caught the eye of church authorities.

If there has been a religious revival in America since the first World War I, one reason for it has been the greater number of chaplains of all churches in the colleges and in the military. If there has been a religious recession, it has at least been slowed down by these same chaplains. Their presence since World War I is a new factor influencing church statistics. Before the increase of chaplains, many young people never saw a clergyman after they left home for college or the armed services. From 1917, physical propinquity to preachers was possible, as it had not been possible since 1870, when higher education first began its fantastic expansion. If from the beginning there had been a comparable increase of the ministry to match the increased numbers of young people away from their home churches, more good would have been accomplished, but at least a beginning has been made.

Actually no one has certain statistics on how Epiphany outreach has been going, or whether or not there is a religious revival. "Whither-are-we-drifting-by the count?" had better be asked half humorously, because it cannot be answered by any tools of research readily available. In student discussion groups, questions are often prefaced by contradictory premises: "Sir, since we are in a religious recession . . ." or, "Sir, since we are in a religious revival . . ." Whichever assumption is made, it should be challenged, if only to teach respect for mathematics. A phrase like "the post-Christian era" is an opportunity to launch a historical digression showing that the faith has had many ups and downs since it began with Abraham and Melchizedek, his priest (*Genesis* 14:18). Samson pulled down the Philistines' temple during a religious recession (*Judges* 16:28–30); Jezebel practiced her whoredoms and witchcrafts in another (*2 Kings* 9:22), and Galatia was post-Christian when Paul wrote his heartbroken "O foolish Galatians, who hath bewitched you?" (*Galatians* 3:1).

For church statistics to convey information, every congregation should be put into one of three groups: those losing ground, those holding their own, and those gaining. The practice of lumping the three together and comparing the single total with population growth gives the meaningless percentages that are published annually. It is only when each group is looked at separately (the losing, the holding, and the gaining) that the figures tell anything.

There is no help for parishes with ineffective leaders until better ones can be found. Mark Twain said there were lyceum fillers and lyceum emptiers, and his distinction also applies to the clergy. No one needs arithmetic to know that congregations will go down where there are poor ministers, what John Milton called:

Blind mouths! that scarce themselves know how to hold
A sheep-hook, or have learned aught else the least
That to the faithful herdman's art belongs!
What recks it them? What need they? They are sped;
And when they list, their lean and flashy songs
Grate on their scrannel pipes of wretched straw,
The hungry sheep look up, and are not fed,
But swollen with wind, and the rank mist they draw,
Rot inwardly, and foul contagion spread.

That leaves the two other groups of churches—those holding their own and those gaining ground. The pastors of these two can be classified as the chaplains of Notre Dame's two-platoon football team were: a defensive chaplain and an offensive chaplain. Some clergy are defensive, temperamentally incapable of advance; nevertheless they may be saintly men who do their part by holding a parish steady. We thank God for them but concentrate research on those congregations with offensive clergy, for only in such churches can the effect of the Gospel be seen. Offensive clergy ask not what is, but what might be; they can build up any church if people live near it, and near is a long way with the automobile. Emerson is often quoted as having said that if a man make better shoes, preach a better sermon, or build a better mousetrap, though he build his house in the woods, the world will beat a path to his door. (Whether or not Ralph Waldo Emerson ever said it, our attributing this remark to him is evidence that people believe it was said by a shrewd observer of life.)

There is no question about spiritual wistfulness, and there never has been: "Jesus . . . was moved with compassion toward them, because they were as sheep not having a shepherd" (*Mark* 6:34). If people are ready to hear and have a minister able to minister, and their church is still not going forward, that data would have astonishing significance. Going forward does not mean by temporary enthusiasms but by the highest criteria. If such standards are used and show that a faithful priest cannot win people for God, the situation would prove that human nature has basically altered.

Christianity has always been winning or losing, now and then, here and there, on a large or small scale. There was a time when it consisted of twelve men; then, in the round numbers used by the Bible, it grew to 70, 120, and 5,000 people, and finally was reduced to One on a cross. If this sounds like poetry, the prose is that a remnant of people will hold to what is true no matter whether the graph goes up or down; faith is independent of fashion or numbers. "*Hier stehe ich! Ich kann nicht anders. Gott helfe mir!*" was said in 1520 at the Diet of Worms by a lone monk in German, but it has been expressed in uncounted languages before and since. "Here I stand. I cannot do otherwise. God help me!"

The difficulty of religious statistics is that they flow like quicksilver. We no sooner get it fixed in our minds that China is leaning toward Christianity than the churches seem to be wiped out by the Communist takeover of 1949; we think Puerto Rico is a religious backwater, but this situation alters in 1940 with the coming of Pentecostal folk; we know New England was Puritan for two hundred years, and is not now. We are amazed to find change in religion although we expect it in everything else—real estate, women's hemlines, government policy. Perhaps this is because the Bible says God is changeless, and the gates of hell shall never prevail against His Church. But the Bible also has a breathlessness that comes from the way human beings change. The New Testament Epistles were written to parishes that were going up or down; even in those days, success or failure was a daily possibility. Today the sad remark that the churches are half empty could be put more accurately as, "Half the churches are empty, but the other half are filled."

The Holy Spirit is referred to poetically as fire and wind, but prosaically He is seen in a minister who is not so much interested in what a parish is as in what he can do to draw it closer to God. He may pray, "Help me, Lord . . . for the faithful are minished from among the children of men" (*Psalm* 12:1), but "minished" does not bother him, because he is in the unminishing business. The currently fashionable question, "What is the profile of this parish?" is not important; the clergy are supposed to be plastic surgeons. *The Makepeace Experiment*, a novel by Abram Tertz smuggled out of the Soviet Union, where statistics certainly do not favor believers, has this closing paragraph:

> He was only a village priest, but one thing he knew: that even if his church were the last on earth, he must stay at his post on the edge of the world and continue to work for the salvation of impious men—continue to work like an ox, like a laborer, like a king—like the Lord God Himself.

Advent, the Christian New Year

Any churchman suddenly asked, "What comes after Christmas?" would reply, "New Year's," a conspicuous instance of mixing holy days and holidays. He knows perfectly well that his New Year comes before Christmas, not after, and is called Advent. The word is Latin and means *"coming to"* for Christ's coming to the world. The secular New Year lasts a day or possibly only the minute of midnight, December 31, whereas the church New Year lasts a month. This extension of time is all-important because if any fresh start is possible with the New Year it requires time to make ready. January First resolutions become January Third jokes, but an Advent month of trial beginnings might produce lasting results.

New beginnings result from new ideas, or new light on old ones. The four Sundays in Advent have had a traditional idea connected with each one, what might be called four easy lessons in Christian thinking. As we return year after year to the same important truths, we get back "that other calendar that strengthens our steps and confirms our joys." The overall theme for Advent emphasized on the First Sunday is the First Coming of Christ; the next Sunday's theme is the Bible; the Third's is the Ministry; the Fourth's is the Second Coming of Christ.

The first coming of Christ is not so much the circumstances of his birth as the impact of his mature years; it emphasizes not Bethlehem but Galilee. It has no resemblance to a story like Bret Harte's *Luck of Roaring Camp*, the account of a baby's gentle presence softening the rough miners in a frontier town where the last woman had died giving him birth. This story is sometimes used at Christmas to draw attention to the effect on mankind of a helpless babe in a manger, but the scriptural account of Christ tells of a resolute grown-up who changed a world that was rougher than Bret Harte's.

Aldous Huxley gives a truer picture than Bret Harte's of a baby's influence (or lack of it). His historical novel *Grey Eminence* is about a monk in the days of Louis XIV whose influence in the chanceries of Europe was profound and corrupt. His political machinations contrasted strangely with the goodness of his private life—fasting often, traveling always on foot as a penance, spending hours in prayer. The reason for this inconsistency between his public and private life was that his meditations were always centered on the Infant Jesus. He filled his imagination with a baby too young to have a conscience and neglected the grown Jesus whose doings and teachings mirror a righteous God.

How the Advent of one man influenced the world can be appreciated by comparing it with other world-shaking events. Is it still reasonable to divide all time into B.C. and A.D.? One meeting of historians, educators, and journalists thought not, and ranked historic occasions in this order of importance:

First: Columbus's discovery of America.

Second: Gutenberg's movable type.

Third: A tie among five events—the airplane, the U.S. Constitution, ether, X-ray, and the coming of Christ.

The First Sunday in Advent poses the question, how would you vote in such a poll?

Freud suggested that two events divided history—the

Copernican and the Darwinian revolutions—and strict Freudians believe there was a third division of history when Freud's ideas became known. They sometimes refer to "the three heavy blows which narcissism or the self-love of mankind has suffered at the hands of science": the Copernican, the Darwinian, and the Freudian discoveries.

Copernicus demonstrated that the earth went around the sun, displacing an earlier astronomy which taught that the sun went around the earth. One result was to show that the universe is larger than man ever thought; the earth is only a speck of a vast cosmos. It may be questioned whether this discovery had the shattering effect on history that Freud thought it did. In the years following 1543, the date of the publication of *De Revolutionibus Orbium Coelestium*, church services went on, young men sought Holy Orders, promises were kept, and the poor were fed, even though the universe seemed suddenly to expand. There was no more difference between pre-Copernican and post-Copernican religion than there was between religion before and after the landing on the moon. Whatever is discovered about the orbits of the planets, the universe is always found to be larger than was thought ten years earlier. An astronomy teacher was fond of saying to his pupils after their first look through a telescope, "never again have a two-by-four idea of God."

Darwinism was the second news that shook human pride, according to Freud. In 1859, Charles Darwin demonstrated that man was not created in a twinkling but through a long evolution from simpler forms of life. Again, it would be hard to prove a loss in religion after Darwin—the nineteenth century showed the greatest missionary expansion Christianity ever had. The new discoveries of biology were gradually absorbed into the framework of faith. They do not deny that God created man; they alter the time span and the method. As popularly understood, however, they raised disconcerting questions. Is man a body only, as some thinkers infer from Darwinism, or does the smallest step in mind make him different? It was upsetting to be reminded so sharply of the *body* in soul-body even though the Bible insists on the body as much as Darwinism does. But man's kinship with animals may be missed in the Bible, because there his difference is so strongly stressed. The Bible holds to the double truth that man is cells among cells, yet unique.

Whatever effect Freudianism had on history came within present memory. Certainly it produced misgivings, but did the Church reel and stagger after Freud, as he thought it did after Copernicus and Darwin? Psychoanalysis has not produced a tide undermining the Church; there are Christian and Jewish Freudians as well as atheistic Freudians. "How did religion survive Freud?" brings a Yankee answer, "How did *your* faith survive? You lived through it all." In one often repeated oversimplification, Freudianism is said to teach that we are more influenced by hidden persuaders than by conscious goals, and therefore are frequently at the mercy of nonrational factors. Freud did not teach this and certainly did not initiate it. Long before he lived, such "Freudianism" existed among thinkers of ancient Greece. Ever since 500 B.C. thoughtful people have faced the determinist theory that man is unknowingly a puppet, not responsible for religious or ethical choices.

There are, of course, many more than these three history-dividing ideas. One, mentioned earlier under baptism, was made popular in the eighteenth century by Rousseau. He painted a persuasive image of the Noble Savage leading a good life until corrupted by civilization. His was a revival of an old idea and went directly against the Bible thesis that man from his earliest state suffered a bias toward evil. Anthropology and everyday life prove Rousseau wrong and the Bible right. Man has a disposition toward evil, what theology calls Original Sin. John Henry Newman wrote, "The human race is implicated in some terrible aboriginal calamity. It is out of joint with the purposes of its Creator."

Karl Marx and Friedrich Engels embraced Rousseau's Original Virtue theory with an enthusiasm that contributed to the false hope of Communism that sin and human perversity would cease as soon as private enterprise disappeared. From this background, Marxists derive a fifth time-dividing revolution, their 1917 Soviet one. "I have seen the future, and it works!" proclaimed one American in Moscow in those days, but events are beginning to show that the succession of ideas was more military than philosophical. It was not Rousseau-Darwin-Freud-Marx but Napoleon-Mussolini-Hitler-Stalin.

Another revolution was set off by Sören Kierkegaard's series of essays on Christianity, a time bomb that exploded a century later as existentialism (see Baptism). He wrote profound theology from 1843 to 1855 under titles that have surprisingly passed into popular speech. So a recent cartoon can show a football player being interviewed by a television crew and quoting titles of Kierkegaard's essays to explain his team's success: "Our defensive line achieved something near its potential. Heretofore we were filled with *Self-Doubt, Anxiety, Fear and Trembling,* and *The Sickness unto Death.*" Kierkegaard wrote in Danish, and delay in translation accounts for part of the long wait before his ideas became widely known. Their sudden emergence after World War II may have resulted from their use by French intellectuals of the underground resistance in the days of the 1940–1944 German occupation. Kierkegaard had taught that no matter how a man is trapped in circumstances, he can escape meaninglessness by deciding for God. This Bible truth about choosing God was altered in the Occupation as a call to choose anything, never mind what. Just decide. Stop hesitating. Kill a sentry. Derail a train. Make a bomb in the cellar. By doing anything decisive you discover your *existenz.*

After the war, the existentialism of the dark days of Vichy had a sudden wide application among both theists and atheists. "Existentially speaking" has become a conversation opener as commonplace as "psychologically speaking" or "statistically speaking," even though not all users are sure what it means. Their best recourse is to keep going back to the original source from which Kierkegaard derived existentialism: "Choose you this day whom ye will serve" (*Joshua* 24:15); "If any man will do his will, he shall know of the doctrine" (*John* 7:17).

Another revolution that is still in progress, mass production, becomes clearer with every trade exposition. Its promise was sung at the New York World's Fair in 1964–65:

> There's a great big wonderful tomorrow
> Shining at the end of every day.

Air conditioning and the like do bring a great big wonderful tomorrow to the masses, and more people can have more goods more cheaply because of Eli Whitney's cotton gin and Henry Ford's assembly line. The industrial revolution may have had more impact than the political revolutions of America, France, and Russia. About factory development, the late Jacob Bronowski said, "The good life is more than material decency, but the good life must be based on material decency."

A revolution prophesied for the near future is the scientific exploration of inner space to match the exploration of outer space. The argument is: now that man has landed on the moon and put devices on Mars, research will turn inward to the mind, the billions that went into satellites will go into psychology. The actual sequence is the other way round. Inner space was mapped long before man could venture into outer space. Freud was asked once why his discoveries came so late in time if they were so important, and he replied that the poets have always known these things. Men understood the human heart before they knew much about science. The Ten Commandments antedated the wheel, in a manner of speaking.

Did the first coming of Christ bring a greater change into the world than these eight revolutions added to the seven of the opinion poll? Is what Jesus said true, "I, if I be lifted up from the Earth, will draw all men unto me" (*John* 12:32)? Marx, Freud, and other original thinkers have been widely lifted up and have failed to draw all men. Will Christ? Was his life the greatest world event, so that *Before Christ* and *Anno Domini* mark the ultimate division of history?

Christians discouraged over how little B.C. and A.D. seem to matter in their family or office can take heart from the astronomer whose janitor thinks the earth is flat and the Freudian who cannot get his sick cousin to a psychiatrist. How can believers be surrounded by pre-Christians, pre-Copernicans, and pre-Freudians? What change does any thought revolution make in history? And, finally, what difference did the First Coming make?

Advent II: Reading the Bible for a Better Year

Once there was a retired clergyman who owned a big yacht (perhaps the only one who ever did), and in conversations on board the Bible would occasionally be mentioned. He always kept one among the slick magazines on deck, and he would thrust it on an unsuspecting guest as if it were a new novel. "This is what we are talking about," he'd say. "You see, it is divided into verses with numbers in front. The author was not Mr. Gideon nor Saint James. The James was a king who had a translation made around Shakespeare's time. Oh, it's quite old; the earliest part was written four thousand years ago in Hebrew. The new part, two thousand, in Greek."

He would rattle on pretending his victim had never seen a Bible before. The joke was that some of his guests never had, a few knew it quite well, and others fell in between. What proportion knew what would be interesting data, not only in the mixed companies on the fantail of that yacht but also among coal miners, undergraduates, Soviet citizens, street people, residents of the Bible Belt, and—let's face it—the clergy. Knowledge is spotty in every group, even among ecclesiastics. The phrase "Biblical theology" has puzzled laymen, who supposed that theology was always Biblical. In theory this is true; the Bible has always been the one essential book for Christians, the center of their thinking. Yet it was not so long ago that Karl Barth and his followers recovered a new awareness of the Bible for Protestants, as Pope John XXIII did for Roman Catholics. Until Vatican II, Latin culture, in both the old World and the New, had little knowledge of it; Robinson Crusoe finds a Bible in his sea chest, but in a corresponding Spanish classic, Don Quixote has none among his books. This is another straw in the wind showing why the Bible ethic of work became known erroneously as the Protestant ethic. Ignorance of the Bible is a staple joke of the comic strip *Peanuts*. Once when Charlie Brown exposed Lucy's astonishing lack of knowledge, she said, "I'm either going to have to sock him or go back to Sunday school."

Reading the Bible is supremely important because it brings what I have called Encounter, with a capital E. Christ will stir a reader now as he did his Palestinian world long ago. The book's theme is renewal, "As the Bible boyishly says, New every morning, and Fresh every evening" (Emily Dickinson). So on one of Advent's Sundays (the Second), Christians ask themselves for the new year ahead: how can I find the treasures of the Bible for myself and my children? The answer is, by reading it doggedly.

If you get up early, good. But if you need every minute of sleep and have to hurry through dressing and breakfast to get to work, fifteen minutes at coffee break is more certain and healthier; or if you are home, fifteen minutes after doing the dishes and making the beds. The evening might be better, although some people's evenings are as rushed as other people's mornings. Read the Bible with your spouse if you can, plus the children, in spite of differences in age and temperament. In any event, start with yourself and persist through eager days and dull days.

I hesitate to suggest practical steps because they immediately evoke reasons why this or that simply cannot be done. When I hear such objections, I get cranky, and blurt out, "(Expletive deleted), figure out for yourself what time you can use. I just say that if you do not read the Bible steadily you cannot be a Christian." In Hebrew the special sense of faith is faithfulness. "The just shall live by his faith" (*Habakkuk* 2:4) suggests doggedness (Fido, fidelity), as do many passages in *Isaiah*, where faith is primarily steadfastness toward God. In Islam, partly a Bible religion, the believers are called "the faithful." For Christians, Bible reading is a chief discipline, like physical exercise and churchgoing; all three may begin as chores and in time become pleasures.

That daily quarter of an hour, for now forty years or more, I am sure has been one of the greatest sustenances and sources of calm for my life. Of course, *such 'reading' is hardly reading in the ordinary sense of the word at all.* As well could you call the letting a very slowly dissolving lozenge melt imperceptibly in your mouth 'eating'. Such reading is, of course, meant as directly as possible to feed the heart, to fortify the will—to put these into contact with God—thus, by the book, to get away from the book to the realities it suggests—the longer the better. And above all, perhaps it excludes, by its very object, all criticism, all going off on one's own thoughts as, in any way, antagonistic to the book's thoughts; and this, not by any unreal (and *most dangerous*) forcing of oneself to swallow, or to 'like', what does not attract one's simply humble self, but (on the contrary) by a gentle passing by, by an instinctive ignoring of what does not suit one's soul. This passing by *should be without a trace of would-be objective judging*; during such reading we are out simply and solely to feed our own poor soul, such as it is *hic et nunc*. What repels or confuses us now may be the very food of angels; it may even still become the light to our own poor souls in this world's dimness. We must exclude none of such possibilities, the 'infant crying for the light' has nothing to do with more than just humbly finding, and then using, the little light that *it* requires.

I need not say that I would not restrict you to only one quarter of an hour a day. You might find two such helpful. But I would not exceed the fifteen minutes *at any one time*; you would sink to ordinary reading, if you did. (Baron Friedrich von Hügel.)

In Bible study the difference is especially clear between God and information about God. If you read the book as God's Word (capital W), it speaks differently from the way it does if you read it as beautiful English, ancient history, or theological subtlety. To be understood, the Bible has to be read on one's knees (metaphorically, not literally, which would be too uncomfortable and distracting). But at the start you can pick it up like a magazine on the clergyman's yacht. The Word is not like ordinary words on a glossy page but "quick, and powerful, and sharper than any two-edged sword, piercing even to the dividing asunder of soul and spirit . . . and is a discerner of the thoughts and intents of the heart" (*Hebrews* 4:12). Two-edged swords are now seen only in museums, but the risk of reading the Word can be understood by thinking of the two-edged razor blade that many shavers handle cautiously every day. The Bible should have written across its cover the word *Dangerous!*

You will come on chapters that do not seem to have anything for you. You plow through, skipping, like a placer miner who takes the big nuggets first and then goes back over the discarded ore for more gold. If a story seems to say nothing in the beginning, it may later speak volumes. Super-progressive education used to say that the child should not hear about the Good Samaritan until after he has helped a mugged pedestrian; only then should he be hurried home to read the story. But parents might look for years without finding a Coat of Many Colors, a Burning Bush, a Golden Calf, a Woman Taken in Adultery in the Very Act. It is occasionally wise to linger on what appears to be unintelligible, because that may be where there is a deficiency in feeling or thinking.

Reading the Bible in a foreign language throws light on the English. Clarence Day pointed out the pleasure of discovering *bienheureux sont les débonnaires* (extremely happy are the debonair) for "blessed are the meek" (*Matthew* 5:5). Comparing modern translations with traditional ones is also valuable, and editions can be found that print them side by side. Most people in their lifetime use a jumble of versions, among them: the King James (1611), the earlier version of the Psalms (by Coverdale, 1535) in the *Book of Common Prayer*, the New English Bible, and J. B. Phillips's modern paraphrase.

Another help to understanding is a commentary that explains every verse. Commentary is available in as many as thirteen volumes, but a one-volume edition will do. It should have an informational tone and provide insights rather than technical analysis. Every generation will have fresh books that map the inexhaustible mine of Holy Writ. The important thing for each person is to find those books that "speak to his condition," as the Quakers say. Faithful

readers finally discover the joy of reading and add their
own marginal comments all their lives.

The Bible can be read cold, but is clearer when inter-
preted, and of course this means with scrupulous accuracy.
By the Middle Ages, inaccurate interpretations had smoth-
ered much of the original sense. To guard against this danger, the Anglican Church prefaced public Bible reading by
the phrase, "Here beginneth such and such," and, with no
comment, "Here endeth the lesson," like quote and un-
quote. The Puritans disapproved of this as "dumb reading"
and insisted that explaining scripture was essential. Their
famous two-hour sermon in colonial days was actually a
one-hour sermon preceded by a one-hour Bible lesson.
Many Protestant churches still have an adult Bible class
before every Sunday-morning worship. I repeat, the teaching must be as accurate as scholarship can make it. That is
why America's first settlers founded a college almost as
soon as they got here, "dreading to leave an illiterate minis-
tery to the churches when our present ministers shall lie in
the dust."

If the Bible is sometimes hard to understand, the reason
is not that it is only for the educated. The ex-pickpocket in
a Salvation Army street band playing "What a Friend We
Have in Jesus" reads the same Bible as the scholar on the
corner waiting for the traffic light and humming Bach's
"Jesu, joy of man's desiring." Both experience the same
Word; the atheist driving by them is wrong in thinking that
the ignorant believe stupidly and the educated evasively.
That idea is the conceit of culture.

An inquirer who wants to go on into Biblical scholarship
beyond his devotional reading will learn which books were
written first, what motives colored certain writings, and
where there are copyists' errors, crude morality, mytholo-
gizing, primitive traces, and signs of development. But he
will also see that beginnings do not reveal the end; em-

bryology is not a substitute for explanation. He may come to the view of E. V. Rieu, an agnostic scholar who made a new translation of the four gospels from the Greek:

> Of what I have learned from these documents in the course of my long task, I will say nothing now. Only this, that they bear the seal of the Son of Man and God, they are the Magna Carta of the human spirit. Were we to devote to their comprehension a little of the selfless enthusiasm that is now expended on the riddle of our physical surroundings, we should cease to say that Christianity is coming to an end—we might even feel that it had only just begun.

Advent III: Recruiting for the Ministry

Concern about the ministry is a third preparation church-men make for the New Year. Not what present to give their preacher for Christmas (if any), but what answer to these questions: "How then shall they call on him in whom they have not believed? and how shall they believe in him of whom they have not heard? and how shall they hear without a preacher? and how shall they preach, except they be sent? as it is written, How beautiful are the feet of them that preach the gospel of peace, and bring glad tidings of good things!" (*Romans* 10:14–15).

No one goes into the ministry without hard thinking; he may even have to do it in spite of opposing influences from those closest to him. Jesus's family is often called the "Holy Family," which suggests absence of tensions. But he burst out once with, "Who is my mother? and who are my brethren?" (*Matthew* 12:48). When he quit being a carpenter to begin preaching, he met opposition from his own circle: "And when his friends heard of it, they went out to lay hold

on him: for they said, He is beside himself" (*Mark* 3:21).
But He did have the support of a second cousin, John the
Baptist.

At family times like Christmas, church people are proud
of relatives who are clergymen; Highland Scots want a son
in the Kirk and Irish Catholics one in the priesthood. There
are exceptions: parents who hope their children won't take
drugs or become matrimonially interested in the wrong
person but are disturbed if a son or daughter considers
becoming a missionary. The attitude is: enough religion to
keep them out of trouble, but not too much. Yet Christians
who take Advent seriously do think of the ministry while
they sing carols and look in store windows. They wonder
whether they would want their children to try the seminary
and whether their own colleges or parishes are providing
their quota of clergy. In trustees' meetings when their pulpit is vacant they expound from years of boredom on the
need for good preachers, but they take little action. It's like
Mark Twain's remark about the weather: everyone talks
about it, but no one ever does anything. So a group of
church people recruiting men for the ministry nicknames
itself the "Weather Club" as a spur to doing something.

The ordained person comes from the average run of people. The whole family may have worked happily in a flour-
ishing parish or patiently in a broken-down one. On the
other hand, he may have only known the church as the
place where his sister got married or where his playmates
took him to Sunday school because his parents never bothered. In school and college his teachers were a mixture of
idealists and time-servers, and his parents saw the influence
on him of each kind. They were pathetically grateful when
they found one whose purpose was "instructing Youth, not
only in . . . those Sciences, wherein they are commonly
taught; but more especially to learn them the *Great End
and Real Business of Living.*" This eighteenth-century

statement of Andover and Exeter Schools might be rewritten: "but more especially to teach them how to get with it, to avoid the identity crisis, or in old-fashioned language, to serve God and country." In every century there will be fresh words, but the experience of being set on fire by a teacher is the same.

Churchmen pray for their ministers every Sunday and especially at the Ember Days, which come in the spring, summer, autumn, and winter. *Ember* is a corruption of the Latin for "four seasons," a popular name for gourmet restaurants around the world. It might be appropriate to call them Ember restaurants so the diners would be reminded that people are needed for the ministry. The winter Ember Days in Advent jog parish ministers into saving time during the Christmas holidays, as busy dentists do, for young people home from college. Ministers often preach on the ministry during the vacation. Apart from the holidays, many churches never meet the future, because youth are not in their home parishes most of the year but are away being educated.

Advent concern for the ministry is not a soothing meditation: the leading colleges turn out doctors, lawyers, and businessmen, but not their proportion of clergymen. In 1967, a study of the Protestant Episcopal Church, under the chairmanship of President Pusey of Harvard, showed that a high percentage of the clergy came from limited educational backgrounds. They were graduates of unaccredited colleges, had low marks as undergraduates, took no part in athletics or other student activities, and would not have been admitted to a good law or medical school. The report proved that the Church is failing to challenge its brightest young people to the ministry; in the Biblical phrase, it is not calling them. In intelligence, the pew in many a parish has outrun the pulpit.

At Christmastime young men argue about why they

should *not* go into the ministry. I don't know why I keep saying young men, for there are many full-time ministries for women and older people, and in actuality all Christians should be included. Farfetched as this sounds, it is true, because every Christian in theory is already in ministry. He must decide why he should not be in the *ordained* ministry. An important by-product of considering ordination is that a person will be more serious about whatever life work he does follow. The long, long thoughts of youth should make him wonder in what sense God could possibly have a vocation for everyone so that no one has to become a peppercorn and drift into what for him is a meaningless job. "Blessed is the man who has found his life work, let him ask no other blessedness," said Carlyle. Chancellor Bismarck once made a commencement speech that was only two sentences long: "There are seven hundred of you graduating here today. Only seventy of you will ever amount to anything." Afterward, when the astounded listeners ventured to ask what he meant, he said, "Seven hundred? Seventy? Ten percent? That's right. Only ten percent ever find their life work; the rest do any old thing" (*Unbedeutenheit*, a German equivalent of the peppercorn).

Research on American workers reinforces this very point, that far too many of them are bored with their daily round, blue-collar and white-collar alike. Only a minority are extremely happy. The explanation lies in the grim fact that Bismarck rudely brought out: only ten percent ever find their life work. The groundswell of dislike of work begins with wrong choice. Of course some young people have jobs forced on them by poverty or lack of opportunity, but in our society, most are free to choose and yet have no idea how important it is to find a satisfying occupation. Popular thinking limits a "calling" to fields like the arts, medicine, and the ministry, which is too bad. Every task from parking-lot attendant to research scientist can be a God-given vocation. If this sounds like a dream, it becomes a reality every year at Advent-Christmas-Epiphany, the seasons that say God was once a schoolboy, a carpenter, a doctor, a teacher and preacher, and that His children are meant to labor joyously, not to drag out their lives in some daily treadmill. When President Kennedy called for more men in public service, he quoted Gertrude Stein's *Brewsie and Willie*: "You'll be old and you never lived, and you kind of feel silly to lie down and die and to never have lived, to have been a job chaser and never have lived."

Advent IV: The End of the World

The first Sunday in Advent says harshly that the Incarnation was not the coming of a baby into human affairs but of a grown person. The fourth Sunday has another harsh meditation about this adult—his Second Coming, which will end the world. Thinking about it can be muddied by efforts to prophesy when it will occur, a speculation expressly forbidden by the Bible. The prohibition arose because some of the first Christians predicted that the end was coming soon, and since time was running out they never married (*1 Corinthians* 7:29); others for the same reason, practiced communism, holding all their goods in common (*Acts* 4:32). The Trump of Doom still appears in stage and cartoon jokes, but the laughter is nervous because everyone knows the world is bound to end sometime, perhaps tonight. It will happen through a nuclear explosion, a takeover by the insects, or the dehumanizing produced by Big Brother in *Brave New World*. In one form or another, Gabriel's trumpet will ultimately sound.

The Second Coming is sometimes explained away as Christ's coming into men's hearts one by one all through history. This is happening, of course, but the Second Coming as sung and preached in Advent is not only this subjective experience but also an objective event that will end history itself. No scientifically knowledgeable person doubts it will take place; the only uncertainty is what comes after. Nothingness? Life something like earth life on another planet? Will some leader of the past return and gather all the multitudes of the human race in a new existence somewhere? If so, who will it be? If not the Christ of our tradition, will it be Rousseau, Thoreau, Jung, or an Asian guru or African statesman who is now proclaiming himself the Messiah?

And most puzzling, in what sense will He "judge" the world? To judge is a metaphor; it does *not* mean what an official does in a law court sitting behind an elevated desk wearing a black gown. It means, what life style survives, and what finally disappears in eternity? Christ's second coming will establish for all time His way of life as the climate for eternal existence. Those who are unhealthy in such a cosmic environment will become extinct, as did the dinosaur in his earthly environment. They will come to what the Bible calls the second death (*Revelation* 2:11; 20:6).

Talk of the end of the world raises the specter of two deaths, the first in this world, the second in the next. For this reason Advent has somber overtones to an age that manages to keep out of sight any death—first or second. Dead horses are no longer seen on the streets, and dead persons are sent to funeral parlors. The obituary formula of one magazine was disconcerting: "Death, as it must to all men, came last week to . . ." People do not die any more, they "pass." Thornton Wilder suggested that murder mysteries are popular because they make dying less formidable by bringing it into midnight reading. "Stroke the nice tiger; see, he won't hurt you!" A former president of Dartmouth College declared that the present generation is disadvantaged because it grew up in homes where the children never saw an elderly relative slowly dying on a makeshift bed in the parlor. Today's children are never aware of drawn-out illnesses, because such sights are hidden in hospitals. Contrary to all this evasiveness, a churchgoer faces steadily the fact of death (possibly the wildest reason of all for going to church!). He is reminded every Sunday that someday his life or the whole world will end, unsentimental alternatives that he grows accustomed to. When death and doomsday are taken for granted, they are not depressing.

Consider the identification disks familiar to members of the armed forces and of no use except in the event of a serious wound or death. In addition to name, rank, and serial number, these bits of metal gave blood type for a transfusion and religious affiliation (C, P, or J) for marking a grave on land or a canvas sack at sea with a cross or a star of David. These "dog tags" were made more ominous by the requirement that two had to be worn, one to be buried with the corpse, the other to be forwarded to Authority. Stateside sailors wore bracelets of precious metals on their wrists, but those in forward areas were required to wear the cheap disks on chains around their necks. It was explained matter-of-factly that an arm might be blown off and a bracelet lost, whereas the head was more likely to stay with the body, hence a necklace had more chance of surviving.

The Christian New Year, four Sundays long, is a month of thinking on such apparently distressing subjects, in contrast to the midnight of nostalgia on December 31 when merrymakers pause to sing, "Should auld acquaintance be forgot?" Here is a startling time difference—one month compared to one minute—especially if it is possible to take the *happy* of the Happy-New-Year minute and spread it over the Advent month. Religious happiness is to secular happiness as a month is to a minute. (And now a parenthesis within a parenthesis: I taught mathematics at Lawrenceville School in New Jersey when Thornton Wilder was teaching French, and there began our lifelong friendship which, among other things gave me the theme of this book. One vacation we were walking in Chicago through the Loop when he suddenly turned and shouted over the noise of the trains overhead: "What we believers forget is that no one is happy without God, no one!")

The reason believers are happy is that they know life in God never ends. Death is man's heavenly birthday. (A saint's day is the day he died, not the day he was born.) "The last gasp of Time is thy first breath and man's eternal prime" (Henry Vaughan). Churchgoers expose themselves weekly to this truth and have it so strongly in their subconscious that they cannot imagine how bleak the world is without it. They believe that no matter what happens here, in the next world hopes will be realized, justice done, and above all, loved ones will be seen again. For this consummation the early Christians greeted each other with the Aramaic word *Maranatha*, "Come, Lord." Every Sunday in church Christians say in the ritual, "Christ has died! Christ is risen! Christ will come again!"

Christ is God seeking man, and this truth suggests one more aspect of the peppercorn—how the law uses it. Some law-school professors throw a handful of the tiny peppercorns out into their classes to teach that the smallest thing can be a "consideration" given in exchange for a favor. "For and in consideration of one dollar, receipt of which is hereby acknowledged . . ." is a phrase everyone has seen. The law used to say, "for and in consideration of one peppercorn . . ." When Queen Elizabeth II came for America's bicentennial celebration, she was given 297 peppercorns by Trinity Church, New York. This total was the yearly rental of the property on Wall Street and Broadway, where a church has stood for nearly three hundred years. In all this time, the parish had never paid the annual peppercorn to the Crown and perhaps was getting nervous. The price had been set at one peppercorn a year because the King long ago required only the very smallest return for the land assigned to the Church. Trinity has always been an important parish, its property is central in New York City, and this situation makes the little peppercorn strangely big even though it is the symbol of nothingness.

Which thing is a parable. When I was talking about peace of mind, I mentioned that some men think they are peppercorns when they are not. But even if they are literally nothing in the eyes of the world and in their own, in God's eyes they are always precious. "For the Son of man is come to seek and to save that which was lost" (*Luke* 19:10). This is the heart of evangelism, that the Church turns peppercorns into men because it never concedes that they are peppercorns. (Maybe that is why Falstaff says "peppercorn" and "the inside of a church" in the same breath.) This sense of the value of the human soul always accompanies the thought of the end of the world. Beggars and queens alike stand before God's throne. In the story Jesus told, it is Lazarus, full of sores, who ends in Abraham's bosom (*Luke* 16:19–31).

This teaching of the Last Things is technically called eschatology, a theological word often summed up in one syllable—hope. The solemn fact is that between the hope of heaven and total extinction there are no plausible alternatives, not even the beautiful one in Robert Louis Stevenson's paragraph:

O unwearied feet of mortals, travelling ye know not whither! Soon, soon, it seems to you, you must come forth on some conspicuous hilltop, and but a little way further against the setting sun, descry the spires of El Dorado. Little do ye know your own blessedness; for to travel hopefully is a better thing than to arrive.

"Why is it better to travel hopefully?" a housewife asked facetiously. "Do we never arrive? In the next world will I always be making more beds, washing more dishes, nursing more children?"

More precise than Stevenson's endless travel is C. S. Lewis's metaphor of the classroom in *Letters to Malcolm:*

> You are—as you used to call it in the shadowlands —dead. The term is over; the holidays have begun. The dream is ended; this is the morning. . . .
> And for us this is the end of all the stories, and we can most truly say that they all lived happily ever after. But for them it was only the beginning of the real story. All their life in this world and all their adventures . . . had only been the cover and the title page: now at last they were beginning Chapter One of the Great Story which no one on earth has read: which goes on for ever: in which every chapter is better than the one before.

Or Cardinal Newman's imagery of the end of a journey: "O Lord, support us all the day long until the shadows lengthen and the evening comes, and the busy world is hushed, and the fever of life is over, and our work is done. Then in thy mercy grant us a safe lodging, and a holy rest, and peace at the last." The moments when we can imagine any such consummation come often in Advent, and "are treasurable, while the music lasts. Yet these are only hints and guesses; hints followed by guesses; and the rest is prayer, observance, discipline, thought and action" (T. S. Eliot).

And now it is December 25.

Putting the Mass into Christmas

The year of Jesus's birth is not known exactly. When it was decided in the sixth century to count all history as before or after Christ, an astronomer estimated the year Jesus was born and set it as zero. However, his mathematics was incorrect, and scholars now calculate that Jesus was born in what is our year 6 B.C. To be correct, all dates should be changed by subtracting six from B.C. and adding six to A.D. What this would do to 1066 and 1776 makes schoolteachers quail, so the mistake has to be left. Thus every check we write reflects an early scientific error, which makes some scientists tolerant of early theological errors.

The actual month and day of Jesus's birth are totally unknown. In the fourth century, it was arbitrarily set near the longest night, December 21, to stress that the Light came when the world was darkest. Another reason for selecting the winter date was to take advantage of the pagan festivities held from time immemorial at that season. The current slogan "Put Christ back into Christmas" is an anachronism; it sounds as though he had been crowded out of a celebration begun in his honor, but it is the other way round. The parties began long before he was born. The winter celebration is an old holiday that Christians are trying to make into a new holy day. "What's so Christmassy about going to church?" is a humorous question that the Church has been trying to answer for centuries by taking over five merrymaking customs, three of them pre-Christian.

1. *Parties* are very old; they were held at this time of the year long before Christ because after December 21 the daylight grows longer. The superstitious hailed the returning favor of the sun god, and the philosophical drowned in drink the annual realization that more daylight by itself won't change anything. Later, when the civil New Year was put at January 1, tearing the last leaf off the calendar was a further depressant calling for wine. Whatever the original motives for the carousing, it provided the infant Church with a rough symbol of their happiness in God. Jesus compared his kingdom to a rich man's banquet and to a wed-

ding which a king made for his son. His stories of a Prodi-
gal Son, a Lost Coin, and a Lost Sheep all end with eating
and drinking.

The Church has been trying to add praying to partying.
Christmas is literally Christ's Mass, and to put the Mass
into Christmas is the first step to putting Christ in. Over the
centuries, it has always been a toss-up whether the season
was for worship or for wassailing. At times the holy day
was so dissolute that some churches forbade its celebration.
Some old people in my Cambridge parish could remember
having to attend public school on December 25. In 1824, in
Massachusetts, an Episcopal church scandalized the town
by gathering an orchestra on Christmas Day and singing
Handel's *Messiah*.

2. *Gifts* are another pre-Christian means of forgetting
the depression of cold weather. For *exchanging*, the
Church substituted *giving* to people who cannot give back,
like the poor and the children. The giving is even made
anonymous through Santa Claus, or Saint Nicholas.

> Nicholas, Bishop of Myra's See,
> Was holy a saint
> As a saint could be;
> Saved not a bit
> Of his worldly wealth
> And loved to commit
> Good deeds by stealth.
>
> —*Phyllis McGinley*

A kindly gentleman whom you can never adequately thank
is not a bad childhood introduction to God. The late
Thomas Dooley, a Navy surgeon, became a medical missionary when he saw the privations of the non-Communists
fleeing North Vietnam. At his clinic, he made the natives
pay for treatments in order to teach them self-reliance—an
egg, a chicken, a sack of yams, whatever they could—on

"What's so Christmassy about going to church?"

Drawing by Alan Dunn; © 1962, The New Yorker Magazine, Inc.

every day except Christmas. On that day, medical treatment was free. So his patients called Christmas "Give-Away Day," the best possible name for it. "God so loved the world, that he gave his only begotten Son" (*John* 3:16).

3. *Greens* come from the Druid practice in ancient England of bringing logs and mistletoe into the house at midwinter to warm the unseen spirits believed to inhabit them. The custom spread to the continent and became the Teutonic forest rites the Nazis tried to revive as late as 1935. Anthropologists say Christmas trees may be a throwback to this paganism; a return to the nature worship denounced by the Bible. Fear of it explains the question mark in *Psalm* 121: "I will lift up mine eyes unto the hills, from whence cometh my help?" The question mark is not a copyist's error; it belongs in the original text even though it is omitted in the King James version. The Hebrew poet lifting up his eyes to the hills remembered that the heathen altars were there for a degrading nature worship. What help was in them? None; his help came from the Lord who made heaven and earth. (When I proposed several times that Blue Doming be banned—this is now the third time of asking—I realized that mountains no longer suggest obscene altars.) With greens and scenery, the Christian takeover is reasonably satisfactory.

4. *Cards* are a new Christmas custom. Visits would be better for keeping up with friends, but most people can't afford the carfare and their friends can't entertain them easily. Letters are also better than cards, but they require leisure for longhand, or a secretary. A statesman had his stenographer write every month to two old cousins, clumsily typing out family news so it would look as though he had pecked out the letter himself. A week before he died, a busy theologian complained, "I have so many pressures on me. My letters have been growing each year—sometimes there are twenty-five or thirty a day. I reply to all of them.

I use this office and my secretary only for writing letters. It's the *agape* in me." Lacking secretaries or leisure, people have to fall back on printed cards. Mass-produced, they are the visit of the housebound, the gesture of the shy, the witness of the devout who do not say the words easily. "Christianity got started with the unnecessary letter," said the late P. B. (Tubby) Clayton, whose letters have cheered thousands.

> Never a Christmas morning,
> Never the old year ends,
> But someone thinks of someone,
> Old times, old scenes, old friends.

Christmas cards need not be limited to religious subjects. *Emmanuel* is Hebrew for "God with us" and blesses all of life. The Incarnation has a pitch alongside the world's carnival; both words are derived from *carnis*, Latin for "flesh" —sacramentalism again.

5. *Tinsel* is another new feature of Christmas that came in lately with mass production. Add advertising to tinsel, and the holiday atmosphere sometimes strikes the fastidious as deplorable. It disturbs them that streets are festooned with streamers, loudspeakers blare carols, packages are gift-wrapped for a fee and carolers race through "Jingle Bells" with a cash register jangling in the background.

In defense of tinsel we remember that it comes from the same assembly line that, because of cheapness, is making more things possible for more people. Tinsel comes today to the poorest as the unearthly beauty of Bethlehem came first to shepherds, the lowest-paid agricultural laborers.

When anyone has managed to hold Epiphany steadily in the background of Christmas parties, gifts, greens, cards, and tinsel, it will be said of him, as Dickens said of Scrooge,

"that he knew how to keep Christmas well, if any man alive
possessed the knowledge. May that be truly said of us, and
all of us!"

The holly in the windy hedge
    And round the Manor House the yew
Will soon be stripped to deck the ledge,
    The altar, font and arch and pew,
So that the villagers can say
"The church looks nice" on Christmas Day.

Provincial public houses blaze
    And Corporation tramcars clang,
On lighted tenements I gaze
    Where paper decorations hang,
And bunting in the red Town Hall
Says "Merry Christmas to you all."

And girls in slacks remember Dad,
    And oafish louts remember Mum,
And sleepless children's hearts are glad,
    And Christmas-morning bells say "Come!"
Even to shining ones who dwell
Safe in the Dorchester Hotel.

And is it true? And is it true,
    This most tremendous tale of all,
Seen in a stained-glass window's hue,
    A Baby in an ox's stall?
The Maker of the stars and sea
Become a Child on earth for me?

And is it true? For if it is,
    No loving fingers tying strings
Around those tissued fripperies,
    The sweet and silly Christmas things,
Bath salts and inexpensive scent
And hideous tie so kindly meant,

No love that in a family dwells,
    No carolling in frosty air,
Nor all the steeple-shaking bells
    Can with this single Truth compare—
That God was Man in Palestine
And lives today in Bread and Wine.

            —*John Betjeman*

Seven

PURITANISM

Celebrating Easter Every Sunday

Every Sunday celebrates Easter Day; at least once a week all year Christians ponder the resurrection of Christ. This weekly remembrance helps remove the information noise that Easter is springtime; it is spring, summer, autumn, and winter. To remind themselves of this, one congregation in the north of England sang an Easter hymn morning and evening for fifty-two consecutive Sundays. Passers-by on the dark street would hear strange words coming out of the church on snowy winter nights:

> "Welcome, happy morning!" age to age shall say:
> Hell today is vanquished, heaven is won today!
> Lo! the dead is living, God for evermore!
> Him, their true Creator, all his works adore!

Remembering the resurrection every Sunday includes remembering the crucifixion every Friday. The two are inseparable; yet associating Friday with Sunday suggests at once a devastating putdown, puritanism. This was a name used long ago in England for high-minded living in licentious times. In the present psychological temper, the least hint of self-sacrifice is rejected as masochistic. Anyone who has not yet picked up that word at least has heard that austerity is unnecessary. He has been told that earth's resources are capable of bringing him total comfort, and that self-denial is morbid. Mr. Dooley remarked that "Thanksgiving was founded by th' Puritans for bein' presarved from th' Indyans, an' we keep it to give thanks we are presarved from th' Puritans." Such gibes are like the obstacles Bunyan described in the Progress of his Pilgrim, one of the original Puritans, until at the last in the stream of death, "he passed over and all the trumpets sounded for him on the other side."

> There's no discouragement
> Shall make him once relent
> His first avowed intent
> To be a pilgrim.

The Risen Christ

Recalling Easter every Sunday and Good Friday every Friday exerts steady pressure on the misconception that Christianity is the Sermon on the Mount and only incidentally the crucifixion and resurrection. The truth is just the opposite: unless God raised Jesus after a horrible death, his teachings end in perplexity and the Sermon is a set of impossible standards. The Christian Church began with the resurrection, as each person begins his Christian life with a resurrection.

A distinguished editor who belonged to Alcoholics Anonymous was going down an outside basement staircase to a meeting one rainy night. Being a sensitive person, he was thinking, "This Chapter of A.A. is a crummy bunch, and their wet overcoats will stink." Then the idea struck him, "Who am I to be critical of poor men who have to wear old clothing?" At that very moment, he said, God came to him and he never took another drink.

A woman in the hospital frightened about an operation clutched a calling card on which her minister had written, "Thou wilt keep him in perfect peace, whose mind is stayed on thee" (*Isaiah* 26:3). Soon it seemed to her that God's peace came over her like a blanket pulled up from the foot of the bed.

A wounded soldier in Walter Reed Hospital asked a Red Cross volunteer to read one verse to him over and over: "God keeps faith, and he will not allow you to be tested above your powers, but when that test comes he will at the same time provide a way out, by enabling you to bear it" (*1 Corinthians* 10:13). The young soldier was in such agony that he was biting on a board. For forty-five minutes the repetition went on until he said quietly, "I am still in pain, lady, but Christ helps me bear it."

The editor called it God; the woman, God's peace; the soldier, Christ. Easter calls it the Risen Christ; Pentecost, the coming of the Holy Ghost; Christmas, the Babe born in our hearts. It is often called God's grace. Theology uses Holy Ghost, Son, and Father interchangeably. Under all these names the sense of the presence of God is one experience no matter what it is called. To the classical terms, new ones have been added, like Indwelling Spirit, the Holy, Inner Light, the Wholly Other, *Mysterium Tremendum*, the Numinous, Peripheral Halo, the Over-Against, Ground of Being, Ultimate Reality. Juke boxes sing "The Man Upstairs" and "Somebody Up There Likes Me." Electronic guitars accompany "He's Got the Whole World in His Hands," "I am the Lord of the Dance." In J. D. Salinger's story "Franny and Zooey," Franny says she performs best on the stage when she picks out someone in the audience and acts for that person, and Zooey tells her that in real life Christ Himself is the fat lady in the fifth row. Those repelled by such things should be placated by Baron von Hügel's dictum that fastidiousness is not a Christian virtue.

The bewildering number of names for the sense of God

underscores again how widespread mysticism is. And let us candidly add once more that it is not always desirable. A mentally disturbed patient being admitted to the hospital was asked the routine question, "Has God ever spoken to you?" She answered, "No, I've never been bothered that way." No one can avoid such unintended humor; the serious point is that mysticism is not finally good unless it is Christian. Therefore the best name of all for the sense of God's presence is the Risen Christ because Christ is the clearest picture of God. We can never tell ourselves too often that God is not an Oblong Blur or a bowl of Gray Tapioca.

Many who have experienced the Risen Christ are unaware how they came to know him. They did not decide that the Bible is true and therefore Jesus must have risen; instead they first felt his presence in their lives and then knew that the Bible is true. It confirmed what they already felt inwardly. The resurrection experienced is the resurrection believed. This was the order with the earliest Christians; they did not say, "I believe Christ rose because my uncle told me, who got it from his mother, who knew one of the Apostles," but, "I already knew in my own brain what Scripture declares." Let us say "brain" with Hippocrates once more, that part of man that both loves *and thinks*. Dr. Michael De Bakey, the heart surgeon, replied to the little girl who asked him whether a plastic heart has love in it, "A plastic heart does have love in it, a very great deal of love." If she had been old enough to understand, he might have written her that it is the brain that loves and at the same time weighs evidence; the seat of affection is also the seat of judgment.

The resurrection is verifiable because it happens here and now in our brains as it happened to the eyes and ears of the disciples in Palestine about A.D. 29. We read of the Risen Christ in the garden, in a closed room, by the lakeside, walking with his friends. These stories might be poetical ways of saying they recalled him so vividly after his death that they almost saw him, but Christians believe that the first disciples saw Jesus with their physical eyes. Believers today "see" and "hear" the Risen Christ, but someday they will see and hear him face to face, without quotation marks, as the first disciples did. Will my reader be bored if I repeat that "seeing" and "hearing" in the brain must be authenticated by the improvement of the "seer" and "hearer" in his character and disposition, two other activities of the same brain?

The Upstanding of the Corpse

Jesus's resurrection is sometimes denigrated as "The Upstanding of the Corpse." This putdown is precisely what the creed says by "He rose again"—he stood again as he had stood before he died. God revivified the nitrogen, calcium, and other elements in Jesus's body and gave them additional properties like the capacity to appear and disappear. Believers do not think God will reanimate their physical bodies in the same way, and therefore do not care whether they are lost in an accident or given to a laboratory. They trust God will give them a new body, freed of weaknesses gathered in this world. But this is getting ahead of Easter, which is about Jesus's resurrection, not man's.

Those who have time for scholarly reading on the subject will keep on collecting information. And they will remove information noise like Ernest Renan's theory that the overwrought disciples imagined they saw Jesus because of their love for him. "*Ce qui a ressuscité Jésus, c'est l'amour.*" They will meet the telegram-from-heaven theory, which says that the visions were not self-induced but were sent by God to the disciples' imaginations. Therefore the visions were just as miraculous as if God had brought a physical Jesus back from the dead. Thoughtful inquirers will hear from another school that the empty tomb was a case of mistaken identity; at Easter dawn the women visited the wrong grave, where a stranger they mistook for an angel said, "He is not here: behold the place where they laid him" (the words "he is risen" being a later addition to the story). Thus a "providential falsehood" made them think the tomb was empty when in fact they were not at the right place.

These ingenious stories to explain away Christ's resurrection must face the fact of the empty tomb. Common sense argues that if the tomb were not empty, the body would soon have been found and produced by enemies to disprove the rising. If found by friends it might have been destroyed to add verisimilitude to their tales of the resurrection. But the enemies never produced the dead body, and the friends died for the conviction that he actually rose. It is conceivable that the enemies lost the body or that the friends persisted in a lie, but it is not likely. The empty tomb leads to the greater likelihood that God raised Jesus. The apostles' amazement when Jesus rejoined them is further evidence of the resurrection, for they had not expected it and had absolutely no such hope that would have led them to fantasize it.

Yet faith does not rest solely on such testimony from long ago but on the presence of the Risen Christ in our own lives, however intermittently. Again, the resurrection experienced is the resurrection believed. And to explain it this way does not limit the evidence to the subjective. Objective evidence is present in Christ's influence on history and in the persisting existence of the Church.

> Though with a scornful wonder
> Men see her sore opprest . . .
> Yet saints their watch are keeping.

Arguments over exactly what happened at the resurrection will never end, but they are swallowed up by the sense of the Risen Christ today. This is one of the words that proceed out of the mouth of God, authoritative for those who feel it even dimly. The details of the event long ago can never be known precisely, and no intellectual formulation has ever been required of believers. Perhaps they make the resurrection too easy, as unbelievers make it too difficult. William Temple said to Bertrand Russell that he believed in the resurrection more than the evidence suggested, and Bertrand Russell replied that he believed in it less than the evidence warranted. No theory is necessary—only the good news that Christ was dead, and is alive. "For we were there and He is here: It is always the third day," as Amos Niven Wilder wrote:

> That immovable stone tossed aside,
> The collapsed linens,
> The blinding angel and the chalky guards:
> All today like an old wood-cut.
>
> The earthquake on the third day,
> The awakened sleeper,
> The ubiquitous stranger, gardener, fisherman:
> Faded frescos from a buried world.
>
> Retell, renew the event
> In these planetary years,
> For we were there and He is here:
> It is always the third day.
>
> Our world-prison is split.
> An elder charity
> Breaks through these modern fates.
>
> Publish it by tell-star,
> Diffuse it by mundovision.
>
> He passes through the shattered concrete slabs,
> The vaporized vanadium vaults,
> The twisted barbed-wire trestles.

A charity coeval with the suns
Dispells the deep obsessions of the age
And opens heart-room in our sterile dream—
A new space within space to celebrate
With mobiles and new choreographies,
A new time within time to set to music.

Man's Possible Resurrection

Man's resurrection depends on Christ's, a sequence Christians repeat to themselves in as many ways as they can. They do not hold, as the Greeks thought, that man is naturally immortal, that he lives forever just because he was born, that his soul is indestructible. Instead, because God raised Christ, He may raise us.

To what? To a continuing existence in a body enjoying God, loved ones, and all the company of heaven. Life after death is not like life in this world, but neither is it totally unlike. Cosby Bell, my professor of theology in the Virginia Seminary, used to say that he hoped to go trout fishing in the Delectable Mountains. Saint Augustine wrote, "We shall rest, and we shall see; we shall see, and we shall love; we shall love, and we shall praise."

This future life has been glimpsed by everyone who has known the good life in this world. He believes in immortality because mortality is good, and by good he does not mean health and security but knowing God and caring for people. For the words "Hell today is vanquished, heav'n is won today!" in the hymn, the psychologist would substitute something like "a new factor is put into daily consciousness which heightens it and makes infinite prolongation attractive." Christ first brings eternal life to Dullsville, and this life continues in another world forever. But it starts in this world; mortality is "swallowed up of life" beginning here and now (*2 Corinthians* 5:4). All the way to Heaven is heaven because He said, I am the way, wrote Saint Catherine of Siena.

> Since I am coming to that holy room,
>   Where, with thy choir of saints for evermore,
> I shall be made thy music; as I come
>   I tune the instrument here at the door,
>   And what I must do then, think here before.

> —*John Donne*

Many who doubt life after death do so because they have found no existence on this globe worth prolonging indefinitely. To them immortality is not incredible but undesirable. Thus to anyone who insists he is not interested in mere continuance of existence, Christians say "Amen." For it has to be good existence. "The mass of men lead lives of quiet desperation. What is called resignation is confirmed desperation." Thoreau's observation has been repeated for a hundred years because fresh evidence of it is always coming in.

When a person insists he never thinks about the future life because he is too engrossed with this one, that is indeed the proper priority. But when someone he loves dies, he is bound to wonder about the possibility of continuing existence. The mourner thinks about this not only because of his sorrow, as commonly said, but also because a neglected truth flashes on him that people are important for themselves. Death forces us to see people as persons, not as providers or influences or entertainers. Whatever practical use a friend may have had, his value went far beyond utility; we loved him for himself. Thus we might say, "For all I know that is the end of you," but we would never say, "For all I care, my dear, that is the end of you." Caring will not bring him back, but it makes us reason that if there is any sense to human life, people are not thrown away. What we care for most is not at the mercy of what we care for least.

Stewart Alsop in his last illness wrote *Stay of Execution,* an account of his gallant struggle for life. For years death was always near with its final question, will a man live again? His intimate story contains paragraphs that say no, and other paragraphs that seem to say yes. Having been one of his tennis group, I wrote and thanked him for the book, adding that no matter what he thought, when death came he would be pleasantly surprised. His reply was sent me by his secretary after he died. It was only one sentence long: "I hope that one of these days we'll both be back on the court, and not as spectators." I am sure we will, although not in Washington, D.C.

At Alsop's funeral we sang "God Be with You till We Meet Again," with the old tune and refrain, as it had been sung at gatherings in his family's home.

> Till we meet, till we meet,
> Till we meet at Jesus' feet,
> Till we meet, till we meet,
> God be with you till we meet again.

It was noticeable that everyone in the congregation sang loudly, believers and nonbelievers alike, I don't know why. Faith? Love? At least with hope, the anchor of Paul's trilogy of faith, hope, and love.

Philosopher George Santayana wrote that we do not meet again: "We must see Heaven in the midst of earth, just above it, accompanying earth as beauty accompanies it. We must not try to get Heaven pure, afterwards, or instead." Faith says *yes* to his first sentence, *no* to his second; Christians expect precisely what Santayana says they must not try to get. Heaven is in the midst of earth, as he affirmed, but heaven is also what he denied, pure, afterwards, and instead. Maybe heaven is up in the sky, maybe down, maybe sideways, who knows where? Or whether in any direction if we can understand Einstein? The matter of direction seemed to have been a traumatic question for Bishop John Robinson; it started him writing *Honest to God* when he was feverish in the hospital and led into the so-called Death of God movement, now dead itself.

The sophisticated Christian answers simple-mindedly that heaven is somewhere. "It looks like Switzerland," says the woman who has just died in Wilder's play *A Pullman Car Called Hiawatha*. No matter where, all descriptions of heaven are guesses; golden streets and pearly gates are simply attempts to picture solid constructions. Asphalt would be easier on the feet than gold, and bronze gates handsomer than pearl; but some kind of substantial streets and gates have to be imagined for the hereafter because that is all we know here. White robes appear in the traditional Biblical scenes since they were one of the glorious sights of the holy days, only possible on rare occasions because of the limited laundry facilities of the ancient world. So it is with golden harps; people surfeited with turntables and radios cannot imagine how rare music was. A kindly putdown by the trout-fishing theologian Dr. Bell was that after the five hundredth time we might be bored singing "Holy, Holy, Holy," and casting down our golden crowns around the glassy sea. On the other hand, he'd add that God and friends and music never become monotonous now, why should they later?

Since these joys are experienced in a body here, most likely they will be experienced in a body hereafter. One scholar has said that in the next world he looks forward to eating caviar to the sound of trumpets, which fits the usual Bible description of heaven as a party. A party requires a place in which to hold it, as well as warm bodies; the afterlife is not ectoplasms interacting gaseously. A heavenly state of mind in this world has to be enjoyed at a location, either in a job or on a sailboat or at a concert, and it's rarely achieved without breakfast. The next world is probably as sacramental as this one certainly is: mind/body, psycho-somatic, spiritual/physical. The words at the Lord's Supper, "The body of our Lord Jesus Christ, preserve thy body and soul unto everlasting life," contain a redundancy, *body and soul,* used deliberately to avoid all possibility of misunder-standing. Strictly, body and soul are the same; no one ever saw a soul without a body, and a body without a soul is a corpse. There isn't even any word for soul in Hebrew; the word translated "soul" means "the man himself." C. S. Lewis writes:

> But for our body one whole realm of God's glory —all that we receive through the senses—would go unpraised. For the beasts can't appreciate it. . . . I fancy the "beauties of nature" are a secret God has shared with us alone. That may be one of the reasons why we were made—and why the resurrection of the body is an important doctrine.

In this book, I use interchangeably the resurrection of the body, life after death, the hereafter, immortality, eter-nal life, everlasting life, and the world to come, but they are not the same thing in careful speech. As used indiscrim-inately by Christians, they cover one general idea: good persons survive physically somewhere after death. The Hindu and the Buddhist are talking about something else when they say reincarnation. Theirs is a return to life in this world; not life after death in another world. The orator who talks about heroes being immortal because yonder statues are guaranteed by perpetual cemetery care is not using immortal as Christians use it. They believe the orig-inals of those statues are now alive somewhere and talking. Maurice Maeterlinck wrote that as long as we remember the dead they are alive, but he was playing with the word "alive." In Christian theory, people live on whether they are remembered or forgotten. To say that Woodrow Wilson's ideals will live forever is an uncertain hope, but that he himself could live forever is literally true, as the New Testament uses the phrase.

False comfort is sometimes taken in the notion that even though individuals die, the human race continues; it will survive on earth or on some other planet. This is impossible comfort to anyone with any scientific knowledge; the atomic bomb brought home its falseness. And even without the bomb, families die out; grandchildren do not confer immortality; nor do colleges, buildings, and cities raised as memorials. God confers eternal life on individuals when these other things are perished as though they had never been. Life after death is not absorption into infinity, or a ghost haunting a castle, or an influence continuing in a government, or a portrait dominating a parlor. Christian immortality is the corruptible bodies of those who sleep in Christ being changed and made like unto his own glorious body.

The Judgment

"Whoever speaks of immortality and does not immediately mention the Judgment is himself in danger of the Judgment," wrote Sören Kierkegaard. He is saying that immortality is tied to conduct, that someday good people will be separated from evil people, that human actions have abiding consequences. As Newman expressed it, "Holiness is the condition for future blessedness." It is a dour thought to keep repeating, but I take existentialism seriously. More important, I quote Kierkegaard on judgment to balance what has been obvious from the start: that this is another "peace of mind" book likely to be dismissed along with guru teaching and watery dilutions of Christianity. I do not apologize, because peace of mind is a desperately sought prize. Freud once deliberately understated it: "Much is won if we succeed in transforming hysterical misery into common unhappiness." The psychoanalyst who asked me on the original post card, "What is the information?" is in the inner-peace branch of medicine. He was asking for something he said every doctor knows must be found: what comes after bread? The universal search is expressed in a jumble of ancient and contemporary questions. What do men finally live by? What must they do to be saved? How is identity found? Where is relevance (ugh)? However the question is phrased, it is asked earnestly because the seeker knows that finding or not finding the answer is heaven or hell, now and hereafter.

A hundred years after Kierkegaard's thunderings about judgment, a British author and critic, J. Middleton Murry, wrote a book on hell because he agreed with the great Dane that judgment was a neglected facet of Christian thinking. Murry had just taken Holy Orders (lovely English phrase for ordination) after the death of his wife, Katherine Mansfield, the writer. From such a wise observer of the contemporary European scene, hell was a significant choice of subject.

About the same time, on the other side of the Atlantic, Thornton Wilder was lecturing on Dante to an extension class at the University of Chicago. His series started so badly that in desperation he asked the class in the third lecture if they believed in hell. To his amazement he got a chorus of noes. "No one holds to that stuff any more!" With the students holding this position, Wilder decided he could not possibly interest them in the *Purgatorio* and the *Inferno*. A few nights later he was having supper at Hull House with Jane Addams and her associate, Ellen Gates Starr. Harking back to his Dante class, Wilder asked those social workers if they knew any damned souls. They burst out with stories of dope pushers, pimps, and other instances of contemporary perdition. Fortified with examples from the greatly admired Hull House, Wilder went back to his students and described hell in Chicago, Illinois. From that time on, they became completely absorbed in Dante's descriptions of hell in eternity.

Everyone knows something about hell on earth either from his own experience or from reading; only poets can describe it in the hereafter. Bible stories picture heavenly banquets, with those outside the party weeping and gnashing their teeth (*Matthew* 22:13). This scene was borrowed from Middle East entertaining, where the custom was for the outsiders to howl around the feasting guests; people were even hired for that purpose, like paid mourners at a funeral. The pain of the outsiders was a thoughtful host's addition to the pleasure of the insiders. From this quaint feature of Palestinian hospitality, theology at times has derived the un-Christian notion that part of the happiness of heaven is beholding the misery of hell.

But the point of the Bible illustration is that heaven is a party, and that hell is to decline the invitation and refuse to go. Heaven is to relate; hell is to withdraw. Most important of all, everyone is invited by a Host who goes to endless trouble to find guests: "Compel them to come in, that my house may be filled" (*Luke* 14:16-23).

One of the two earliest Christian creeds says, "The third day He rose again," and adds this qualification, "according to the Scriptures," quoting *1 Corinthians* 15:4. This is not like saying "according to the newspapers," or "if we can believe the radio reports." It means He rose as the scriptures describe resurrection. The early disciples' scripture was the Old Testament, which gives two characteristics when it describes life after death: (1) it is in a body, and (2) it depends on goodness. Bodily resurrection was discussed in the last section. Goodness is brought home by a ludicrous happening once at a funeral. A clergyman had started up the church aisle ahead of the casket, as is customary, reading the great words from John's gospel, "I am the resurrection, and the life" (*John* 11:25). At that moment, another clergyman, who had been expected to conduct the service, rushed in late and embarrassed, pushed the first one aside, and said, "No, no, *I* am the resurrection and the life." Ministers have nightmares over this story, but it drills into their minds that "I" refers to Christ. The promise is not that there is a resurrection and a life, but that *in Christ* there is one. Goodness is a condition. By trying to be good, man may live again through God's gift. By finally destroying God's voice in his mind, he will be in hell hereafter as he was from time to time in this world.

Judgment is simply a word for dramatizing the difference between accepting or declining a party, coming inside or staying outside. The Bible describes other differences, like dividing sheep from goats (*Matthew* 25:32) and separating wheat from chaff (*Matthew* 3:12). City people unfamiliar with such operations have seen on television cattle cut out from a herd for branding. The profligacy of nature illustrates a form of judgment: for every oak tree grown, thousands of acorns are wasted on the ground; for every animal conceived, thousands of cells are spent. Every acorn and cell does not come to the same end. Nor does every human infant survive; and of those who do survive physically, some will not develop mentally, and among those with all their faculties, some will fail to make much of life. Apart from inherited weaknesses or cruel accidents, some well-endowed people, by their own free will, come to the same end as acorns on a city sidewalk. Of course, acorns do not decide to become oaks, or roe to become fish, but when a certain stage in evolution is reached, human beings can decide. A person with a competent brain and body has reached that stage of responsible choice, and of those able to choose now in this world, some select life and others drift into frustration. (For those unable to choose freely because of a handicap, I believe there are new chances in eternity through God's seeking love.) Abraham Lincoln once remarked that he did not like a certain man's face.

"But, Mr. President," someone expostulated, "a man is not responsible for the face he was born with." Lincoln replied, "But this man has passed that age."

These then are a few of the ways to picture the difference that the Bible calls judgment: accepting or declining an invitation to a party, dividing farm produce, the profligacy of nature, evolutionary selectivity, freedom of choice, passing an age. Anyone who says there are no such contrasts has failed to observe the life around him. Put scientifically, to deny the objectivity of value is to adopt "skepticism of the instrument" in so extreme a form as to make all intellectual effort futile. In plain words, it makes no sense at all to say that there are no differences in living and existence is neither good nor evil, that it simply is. This reflection leads to Christian burial, the last of the nine church rites.

Dirge and Dirigible

The Irish have made the funeral a social occasion. For the English it is the wedding; for the French, baptism; we Americans, being a mixed nation, make all three social. Especially at funerals, people who have not seen each other for years are brought together socially, and it is difficult to preserve the solemnity considered appropriate when long-absent cousins greet each other in the house or outside the church. There is a natural curiosity about what has happened to everyone. Has Cousin Maggie's boy fulfilled the promise of his school days? Is Fred's third marriage working out? Has Luke quit drinking? Such a gathering resembles a college reunion, where the unspoken question is, what has life done to the people I have not seen for a long time? More abstractly, what is the best way to live?

Such reflections are appropriate at a Christian burial because the theme of the rite is conduct, not grief. Dirge has come to mean a song of mourning, but its original meaning was a prayer for guidance. It is a contraction of the Latin imperative *dirige* ("direct thou") and has the same root as dirigible, a directable balloon. Medieval funerals began with *Psalm* 5:8, *Dirige, Domine . . . viam meam*, "Steer my way, Lord." A dirge is a song of differences, not of sorrow. The first need of everyone at a funeral is for direction more than comfort. Since we are all going to die, how shall we live?

The nonchurchgoer attending the funeral only out of respect for the deceased may think that the clergyman is taking advantage of a captive congregation to urge virtue. Perhaps he remembers a funeral oration that started innocently, "Friends, Romans, countrymen, lend me your ears: I come to bury Caesar, not to praise him." But the orator did praise Caesar and intended from the start to rouse the mourners to action. Every eulogy turns into "Let the living follow this good example." Abolitionists before the Civil War gave antislavery speeches at funerals, and Quakers today often preach pacifism at the graveside.

Good conduct is the logical basis for the hope of a future life, and this relationship was realized long before Christianity. The cave man reasoned that the afterlife depended upon excellence; no one but heroes went to the Happy Hunting Grounds of the Red Indians, or to the Elysian Fields of the Greeks. The triumphant note in military funerals comes from the implied virtue of heroism. Eternity depends on behavior; a run-over squirrel is not as significant as a dead person, because squirrels do not make moral choices. "I don't care what they say with their mouths— everybody knows that *something* is eternal . . . and that something has to do with human beings" (Thornton Wilder, *Our Town*).

If the discomfort of the pew or the undertaker's folding chair permits further speculation, the stranger may be thinking that tying heaven to heroism is religion's carrot. He thinks he sniffs what Marx labeled a narcotic to keep people docile:

> Work and pray,
> Live on hay,
> And you'll eat pie,
> Bye and bye,
> In the sky.

But, as we have seen, Christianity intends pie in this world as well as in the sky; "Religion is the opium of the people" was not original with Marx; it was first said by an Anglican clergyman and author, Charles Kingsley, whose zeal for social reform in Queen Victoria's England showed that his religion intended pie here and now. And this intention explains why Christianity was able to put over the idea of immortality more vividly than other religions, if I may say it this way. It was not just a case of getting hold of a good thing and stressing it more than other faiths did. Christian immortality was grounded in firsthand knowledge that Christ made life good in this world and therefore desirable in the next.

Sometimes at a burial there will be a eulogy to make the rite more personal and the ethical point perhaps more explicit. The objection to such an address is that human judgments introduce inequalities and in death everyone is equal. Some churches ensure that all coffins look alike by covering them with a pall—that is, a flag or a church cloth (hence the word pallbearer). In this way no one can tell how expensive the casket is. The same thinking may forbid flowers; the quantity of wreaths emphasizes the difference between rich and poor, between the widely known and the friendless, though on the other hand flowers symbolize the possible loveliness of life now and later.

Churchmen prefer simple funerals; they put the body out

of the way, bury it, cremate it, or ease it overboard at sea. Their indifference is in contrast to the concern for dead bodies shown by primitive man, who built tombs before he built houses. Expensive graves go back to the dawn of human life; they survive in the newest communities in America, which have reverted to the oldest customs and give English authors material for satire. The cult of the body beautiful calls for palatial death parlors and elaborately landscaped cemeteries.

At a Christian burial, lavishness is out of place. Advertisements of expensive grave vaults "to protect the loved one from snow and rain" prey dishonestly upon grief, since bodies decompose in the most expensive coffins within five years. So "final resting place" is as meaningless a phrase as the social note that Mrs. Picklepuss has taken up her permanent residence at Splendorville. There is no permanent residence on this planet either in Splendorville or the grave. To impress this healthy honesty on the imagination, a burial service says, "earth to earth, ashes to ashes, dust to dust." In the old days everyone present picked up a handful of earth and cast it on the coffin. This custom is still followed when burying English kings at Windsor. "Sweets to the sweet," a stock phrase for passing candies to ladies, was originally said by the Queen in *Hamlet* as she threw flowers into Ophelia's grave. In America nowadays it is usually the clergyman who casts the earth or flowers (perhaps because dust to dust is too upsetting for the layman); or white sand from a pill bottle, instead of common soil, is sprinkled by the undertaker on the presumption that he alone is hardened to this solemn truth.

If these comments sound carping, it is not because the clergy grow accustomed to funerals. They never get used to them, and they know their importance for purging grief. The Roman Catholic rites for President Kennedy, watched by the whole world on television, "were a redemption, a catharsis, investing the ghastly futility that had gone before with meaning. Maybe that craving for significance is a weakness," adds William Manchester in his *Death of a President*, "yet I doubt it."

No, it is not a weakness, and the craving for significance finds its deepest satisfaction in dirge (*dirige*, "direct me," while I mourn). And with new direction "hearts are brave again, and arms are strong, Alleluia!" The Christian burial rite is not an exercise in stoic acceptance of bereavement. It is a plea for guidance; to thank God for this life that has been taken (such as it was, let us be honest); to pray He will forgive its sins and perfect it in eternity, and that we shall see our beloved again. And we ask, "O God, help us to live nobly, to thine honor and glory, and to the good cheer of our fellow men."

All the Way to Heaven Is Heaven

The celluloid button that asks, "Is there life after birth?" jolts us into a double take because it is a switcheroo on the usual question, "Is there life after death?" Both go back to a much older question, "What must I do to be saved?" (*Acts* 16:30). Commenting on *saved*, Bernard Bosanquet, an agnostic philosopher, writes:

> The old monosyllable, which since the coming of Christ has sounded so clearly the S.O.S. call of humanity, utters, it would seem, an ultimate need. And yet what is it? The old word does not say; and this, I think, is very significant. We are to understand without telling, and I suppose we do.

"Yes, I suppose we do," responds John Baillie, a Christian theologian, explaining to people like myself, who are deficient in the classics, that

Salvation is the Latin *salus* from which comes the English salutary, salubrious, eye-salve, etc., and is cognate with the Greek *holos* and our English whole, hale, health, and with the German *Heil*. . . . St. Peter used another Greek word, *Hygieia*, the goddess of health. If the King James Version rendered *sound doctrine* as *hygienic teaching*, it would be even closer to the original Greek. It sounds very modern to say that faith is the secret of spiritual hygiene, but it is in the New Testament! . . . The Gospel narratives are more redolent of a hospital than a church. . . . The world is sick and needs to be made whole; though we prefer to use a more pedantic word for *whole*, the Latin *integer*. To say our personalities are not integrated makes our condition more respectable.

Yes, there is life after birth as well as after death. There is salvation both here and hereafter, whether it is called *salus*, *hygieia*, health, peace of mind, happiness, or integration of personality. Of these names, the best might be happiness, because its meaning is unmistakable. It is a risky thing to say that Christ died to make men happy, but at least it is clear. Aristotle saw in Plato the relation between happiness and goodness four hundred years before Christ:

> He alone and first of men showed plain for all to see
> By the life he lived, by all the words he ever spoke to
>   men,
> That the good man is the happy man, now, here, upon
>   the earth.

Yeats wrote nineteen hundred years after Christ:

> For the good are always the merry
> Save by an evil chance.

Whenever the Gospel appears gloomy, it is the fault of those who teach it badly. Faith, hope, and love are joyful things when preached accurately. "If churlishness were a virtue, priests would be saints" was an appalling medieval proverb. Jesus's characteristic saying was "cheer up," "be of good cheer" in the King James Version (*John* 16:33). The German pastor Dietrich Bonhoeffer, arrested for conspiring against Hitler, wrote cheerful letters in the very shadow of the gallows. He was described by his fellow inmates in the maximum security prison as bringing back the *hilaritas* of the early Christians.

Four hundred years before Bonhoeffer, Ignatius Loyola and his "Inseparables" of the University of Paris showed the same *hilaritas* in the most solemn moment of their lives. It was the day they went to the church on Montmartre and after Mass swore complete obedience to the Pope and took vows of poverty, chastity, and obedience. On that beautiful summer morning, the Society of Jesus came into being. The Spanish and French brothers rushed out into the sunshine and romped like children; they played prisoner's base, shoved one another into ditches, and climbed, singing, to the top of Montmartre.

Festivitas characterized Sir Thomas More, Henry VIII's chancellor of England and saint of the Church. Constantly beset by difficulties and finally beheaded, he was always adjuring those around him to be festive. The final word about Christians is joy. They throw themselves into the world's work and share its anguish but also possess "the heavenly serenity of those who see things in the perspective of Christ's resurrection" (Michael Ramsey).

Joy, which was the small publicity of the pagan, is the gigantic secret of the Christian. . . . I open again the strange small book from which all Christianity came; and I am again haunted by a kind of confirmation. The tremendous figure which fills the Gospels towers in this respect, as in every other. . . . His pathos was natural, almost casual. The Stoics, ancient and modern, were proud of concealing their tears. He never concealed His tears; He showed them plainly on His open face at any daily sight, such as the far sight of His native city. Yet He concealed something. Solemn supermen and imperial diplomatists are proud of restraining their anger. He never restrained His anger. He flung furniture down the front steps of the Temple, and asked men how they expected to escape the damnation of Hell. Yet He restrained something. . . . There was something that He covered constantly by abrupt silence or impetuous isolation. There was some one thing that was too great for God to show us when He walked upon our earth; and I have sometimes fancied that it was His mirth (G. K. Chesterton).

So I Did and Here I Am!

Paganism begins with a party and ends with a hangover; Christianity begins with a hanging and ends with a party. However glib, this statement says plainly what is primary: that Good Friday and Easter are inseparable. The crucifixion belongs with the resurrection; Jesus's risen body bore the scars of the cross. Celebrating life requires austerity, no matter that it is sometimes dismissed as puritanism. By this time putdowns no longer bother us. Long before the term puritan came into the language, the name Christian itself was scorned when "the disciples were called Christians first in Antioch" (*Acts* 11:26). The name had the same overtones that "Christ-er" and God-hopper" had until recently among undergraduates. Even before Antioch, Pilate's placard, "This is the King of the Jews" (*Luke* 23:38), was fastened over the cross in three languages—Greek, Latin, and Hebrew—so no one in Jerusalem would miss the sarcasm.

The hanging is easier to make fun of than the party, so Friday jokes are more common than Sunday ones. Puritanism is more vulnerable than Sabbatarianism. Christians who abstain from meat on Friday are vulgarly known as "mackerel-snappers." Yet there is a compelling reason for observing diets and seasons given by my Orthodox Jewish friend Herman Wouk. He told me that every time he sat down to a meal he wanted to be reminded of what is most important in life. This is psychologically sound and explains why sophisticated Christians observe Fridays as well as Sundays. Their hymns recall the hanging as well as the party:

"Oft in danger, oft in woe, onward, Christians, onward go."

"In the cross of Christ I glory."

"Were you there when they crucified my Lord?"

"Beneath the cross of Jesus I fain would take my stand."

"When I survey the wondrous cross where the young Prince of Glory died . . ."

"Fight the good fight with all thy might."

John's gospel actually looks forward to the crucifixion, paradoxically calling it Jesus being glorified. Good Friday was a victory; it is *good* Friday. In the course of history, the observance of the day gradually came to include all the preceding week (now known as Holy Week) and ultimately expanded to forty days of self-denial called Lent in preparation for Easter.

Lent is Old English for length and tells us that God's presence could *lenten* (lengthen) in our hearts as daylight *lentens* in the spring. To speak of daylight *lentening* in the spring is another reminder that Christianity originated in the northern hemisphere. Yet, once more, Easter has nothing to do with spring in spite of a recent *New York Times* editorial: "We call it spring, and we celebrate it as Easter and Passover. It is renewal, rebirth, release from the winter of the soul. It is faith and belief triumphant. And it is written in so simple a place as a bursting bud." Good gray information noise! The Passover was an early victory for liberty. Easter was the resurrection of Christ. Both are written in blood, not in bursting buds.

To connect Easter joy with Lenten self-denial makes some Christians fear that the self-denial may obscure the deeper resurrection truth, that God's grace is a gift, not earned by austerity. Such strict constructionists insist that the secret of Christianity is not the will of man but the availability of God. They fear that emphasis on will power can lead to ethical culture or trying to be good without faith. Too much tightening of the belt and pulling up of the socks can verge on noble secularity. They say it is a return to the rigidity of the Law in contrast to the freedom of the gospel. Lent can degenerate into legalism: "I hate my cousin but I'll give up alcohol for forty days." They point out Jesus's scorn for cooks who offer one-tenth of every pinch of seasoning they use in food but are disloyal to Him outside the kitchen. "Woe unto you . . . hypocrites! for ye pay tithe of mint and anise and cummin, and have omitted the weightier matters of the law, judgment, mercy, and faith." They forget Jesus's startling after-remark, "These ought ye to have done, and not to leave the other undone" (*Matthew* 23:23). The passage is one of many that teach us that God's grace is accompanied by man's effort. The Holy Spirit comes to disciplined people keeping Ten Commandments Day; pentecostalism depends on puritanism. Eternal vigilance is related not only to Passover liberty but also to resurrection faith. Lent also celebrates the Risen Christ.

For those brought up to keep it, the childhood memories are as happy as those of Christmas; nothing ever tasted so good as the first chocolate rabbit after forty days of abstinence. Resolutely walking past an ice cream store is remembered later when strength is needed for greater denials. The money saved on sweets went into a mite box and was proudly brought to church to buy a dog team for an Alaskan mission or to furnish medicines to unpronounceable nations. It is worth noting once more how many votes against isolationism come from childish sacrifice for far-off places. The whole family was involved in abstinence; they encouraged each other or watched each other, whichever way you want to look at it; Christians Anonymous again.

Whatever our discipline the rest of the year, Lent is for getting further into its practice. The joy of self-control does not come from reading about soldiers, scholars, and Olympic athletes. It has to be tried at first hand, especially by those who came in late and never had it in Sunday school. Robert Frost's fierceness applies:

> Never give a child a choice. Don't give him a choice of believing in God or not. He can start having choices when he goes to college; they have the elective system there, you know. There's so many courses now where everything you say is right enough—Sociology, Psychology, Contemporary Civilization. I'm at large, and I'm a civilized man, but school is for discipline. A student is an orange pip between my fingers: if I pinch him he'll go far. I'm not violent, but I'm going for the whole damn system. Tightness, Firmness, Crispness, Sternness. . . . Life is tons of discipline.

So much for the child. The adult needs the same tightness, firmness, crispness, sternness, tons of discipline, especially in this present moment of history. Probably he has always needed it, but the urgency now is widely recognized. The argument runs this way: first, the world needs more of what the Bible indiscriminately calls prosperity, wealth, riches, or plenteousness; second, to produce more, everyone must labor harder; third, for a long time to come there won't be enough of these affluent synonyms to go around; and, fourth, those who do have enough must live frugally in order to have more to give away. However cornball (what an eclipsing term!) this sounds, it is being said by discerning people who are not living cornball lives. Their rule is to live simply that others may simply live.

How anyone enters this crucial (from *crux*, "cross") life style has been suggested several times, and perhaps an existentialist story from the Left Bank can say it once more. A Parisian traveling in Tibet was entertained one night at a lama's banquet and was astonished to see across the tent a man dressed in Tibetan pantaloons and golden slippers, at the same time wearing an alpaca coat with a *chapeau melon* (a melon hat, a derby). Recognizing a Paris bank clerk by the coat and hat, he went over to him after the dinner and asked how in the world he ever got to Tibet. This was his story:

> Two years ago I was stopped on the Champs Elysees by a stranger needing a match. As he lit his cigarette, I saw he was a man of the world, so I asked him the question I used to ask everyone—how could I get to Tibet?
>
> "Turn right and go down that street to the railroad station," the man said, "and you will find the train for Tibet."
>
> "Of course," I replied, "but first I will stop at my apartment and pack a bag."
>
> "No!" he said. "Do not delay for clothes."
>
> "You are right, Monsieur, I had better not pick up a bag; but on the way to the station, I will go to my bank and get money for the journey."
>
> "NO!" he shouted. "GO STRAIGHT TO THE STATION AND TAKE THE TRAIN."
>
> So I did and here I am!

The shout on the Champs Elysées matches the shout in my back yard that began this book—DOOM! DOOM led to

CHURCH, and CHURCH (via the concordance) to Shakespeare: "If I have forgotten what the inside of a church is made of . . . the inside of a church!" The shout, GO STRAIGHT TO THE STATION, comes out DECIDE! Quality of life depends on *decision*; no one has to live long to understand that. He uses his will as he grows up in school and in jobs; he forces himself to obey rules; indeed there are hours when all he can do is to hang on to dull obligations. He keeps Good Friday every Friday.

But will power is the lesser part of what a Christian lives by; there come larger hours when he is in love with God and lives gloriously in the strength of that emotion. He keeps Easter Day every Sunday. While he tries harder he trusts more. Finally, Christianity is personal loyalty to a personal Lord.

One Easter Day in Tokyo, I went to a sunrise service held by the tiny Christian community of that largest city in the world. It was drizzly cold with only a handful of people in the amphitheater of an amusement park. We were surrounded by the empty beer cans and paper hats of Saturday night's carnival. My Japanese host, Yoshio Osawa, a boyhood friend from Camp Dudley, took me underneath the stage to meet his Congregational minister, who later read the Bible in the service (actually he recited it because he had been blinded at Hiroshima). Down below, the place was dark and smelled of stale urine and vomit; a Salvation Army band, dressed oddly in Episcopal choir robes over their uniforms, was tuning up for the service. Suddenly they began practicing an Easter hymn:

> Jesus Christ is risen today, Alleluia!
> Our triumphant holy day, Alleluia!
> Who did once upon the cross, Alleluia!
> Suffer to redeem our loss. Alleluia!

Like every old Reservist, I go for a band; the blare of the brass that morning lifted me up from the gloom of the cellar and the pitifully small number upstairs remembering the Resurrection. I returned to my seat and wept all through the service, not a word of which I understood except the Hebrew alleluia (pronounced *hareruya* in Japanese):

Sukue no nushi wa, Hareruya!
Yomigaerishi zo, Hareruya!
Kachidoki agete, Hareruya!
Agame matsure yo, Hareruya!